TAKING YOUR
CHURCH
TO THE
NEXT LEVEL

DEMCO

0   50637 16029   3

Who says marri...   ...selling author Barry Sinroc
and his newlywed dau...   ...behind-the-bedposts peek
at the lives of America's newlyweds in *Just Married*. Based on the recently
completed surveys of 3,876 newlyweds from all 50 states, the book is an
intimate, intriguing, often hilarious look into the world of the newly hitched.

Among the shocking secrets the authors uncover:

83% of the couples kissed on the first date (17% slept together)

11% said at least one of them was a virgin when they got married.
And among virgin couples, 16% were both virgins

72% find their lovemaking better now that they are married

67% shower together

36% have to be kissed in order to make love

31% have made love to a sleeping spouse

70% like to fool around while driving

You'll also learn the fascinating answers to these probing questions:

How many sexual partners have you had in your entire life?
How many do you think your spouse has had?

If you were propositioned, would you tell your spouse?

What is the most unusual way you pamper your spouse?

What's your spouse's best/worst quality?

What was the cheapest wedding gift you received?

What was the real reason you married your spouse?

What is the most annoying thing your mother-in-law does?

In *Just Married*, the authors dare to ask, and newlyweds dare to answer,
the questions that reveal the naked truth about life after "I do."

**Andrews McMeel
Publishing**

an Andrews McMeel Universal company

www.andrewsmcmeel.com

Design and illustration by Tim Lynch

Printed in U.S.A.

$8.95 U.S.A. *($12.50 Canada)*

50895

9 780836 254266

ISBN 0-8362-5426-0

"Gary McIntosh is absolutely right: 'What got you to where you are won't get to where you want to be!' Here's the tool to help you take your church to the next level. Upon reading his helpful book, I kept asking myself: 'Where was Gary McIntosh when I needed him?' I highly recommend *Taking Your Church to the Next Level* to every church planter, pastor, and leader, regardless of the life stage or size of church. Dr. McIntosh provides so much helpful information and insight that this book will not gather dust on your shelf, but will become a well-used reference tool for years to come."

Stephen P. Struikmans, teaching and founding pastor, Rancho Community Church

"In this book Gary McIntosh goes beyond simply identifying the challenges in the church today—he supplies the reader with practical tools to address those challenges. If you have the desire to move your church to the next level and are willing to put in the effort, you will want to read, share, and implement the insights this book offers."

Phil Stevenson, general director of Evangelism & Church Growth of The Wesleyan Church

"Gary McIntosh has presented new ideas to describe the life cycle of the local church. His analysis assists church leaders in understanding what level of life cycle they are in and suggests action initiatives to take to reach the next level of fruitfulness. This book is an excellent resource in coaching pastors and lay leaders on strategies in leading a church to embrace new ways of doing ministry to break growth barriers, and go to the next level."

Ray Ellis, director of the Consulting Network for the Free Methodist Church of North America; senior pastor of Willow Vale Community Church

TAKING YOUR
CHURCH
TO THE
NEXT LEVEL

What Got You Here
Won't Get You There

Gary L. McIntosh

BakerBooks

a division of Baker Publishing Group
Grand Rapids, Michigan

Published by Baker Books
a division of Baker Publishing Group
P.O. Box 6287, Grand Rapids, MI 49516-6287
www.bakerbooks.com

Printed in the United States of America

Library of Congress Cataloging-in-Publication Data
McIntosh, Gary, 1947–
        Taking your church to the next level : what got you here won't get you there / Gary L. McIntosh.
            p.   cm.
        Includes bibliographical references.
        ISBN 978-0-8010-9198-8 (pbk.)
        1. Church growth. 2. Church renewal. I. Title.
BV652.25.M31855 2009
254′.5—dc22   2009022196

Scripture is taken from the New American Standard Bible®, Copyright © 1960, 1962, 1963, 1968, 1971, 1972, 1973, 1975, 1977, 1995 by The Lockman Foundation. Used by permission.

11   12   13   14   15   16   8   7   6   5   4   3

In keeping with biblical principles of creation stewardship, Baker Publishing Group advocates the responsible use of our natural resources. As a member of the Green Press Initiative, our company uses recycled paper when possible. The text paper of this book is comprised of 30% post-consumer waste.

Contents

Contents

1

What Got You Here
Won't Get You There

The significant problems we face today cannot be solved at the same level of thinking we were at when we created them.

Albert Einstein

"I'm glad we could all get together this weekend," Mike greeted Wes and Phil as they settled into three overstuffed chairs at the Holy Grounds, a local coffee shop. "Mary and I are leaving for vacation in a week, and I want to get some input from you two concerning my future at New Hope Church before we leave town."

"Wow! Slow down a bit," Wes said. "The last time we talked everything was going well with your ministry. Has something changed?"

"No, nothing that is worth talking about," Mike replied. "I'm just feeling a bit . . . well . . . it's hard to put into words, but I guess I'm feeling somewhat frustrated with the church's progress."

"What do you mean by the church's progress?" asked Phil. "I'm as puzzled as Wes. Last year you were thinking you'd be at New Hope the rest of your life. What's happened?"

"Nothing's happened exactly," Mike continued. "We're running about 1,150 in worship attendance, and there are no major conflicts. I really should be happy, but ministry just seems . . . so . . . stale. When I started New Hope twenty years ago, I seemed to know what the church needed. The initiatives my start-up team put in place back then took hold, and we doubled and tripled our attendance at worship services in the first few years. Things are still going well, but the last three years we've been on a plateau. We go up a little and then down a little—can't seem to make any solid gains. I've grown more frustrated every year. I just can't figure how to get to the next level, whatever it is."

"Are others feeling the same way?" Phil quizzed. "I mean, does your staff and board sense the same frustration?"

"Yes, everyone feels about the same, but we can't agree on what to do about it," Mike replied, gazing at his coffee cup. "That's bothering me a bit too. When I started the church, there were three members on my planting team, and we were all on the same page. Today I have twelve people on my board, and we never agree on what direction the church ought to go."

"I know what that's like," Phil acknowledged, nodding. "My board is currently trying to decide whether to add a Saturday night worship service or not. We've been going around and around the issue for nearly a year now. I'm about ready to give up on the idea."

Mike smiled as he caught Phil's eye. "We faced a similar situation. Our board presented an initiative to the church to build a new auditorium four years ago, but they voted it down. Since then we can't seem to get a handle on what to do."

"I read somewhere," Wes said, "that churches face predictable barriers at certain sizes. Maybe you've reached one of those barriers."

"It could be, but if our church is stuck at a growth barrier, I certainly don't know what the next steps are to break through it. In fact I'm not even sure there are growth barriers in a church. Remember our speaker at last year's pastors' conference? He said there was no such thing as a numerical barrier. He said all the talk about growth barriers was just a myth."

"Yes, I remember that comment," Phil said, "but the speaker also talked a lot about the effect that a church's age has on its growth."

"Sure, I remember that," Mike said. "I've thought that could be part of our problem too. We celebrated the twentieth anniversary of New Hope's founding this year. As I remember, that is a critical point in the life of any congregation."

"Perhaps New Hope is simply getting old," suggested Phil.

"Well, if that's the case and things don't change," Mike declared, "I'm outta here. I don't see myself pastoring a static church."

This conversation illustrates three aspects of church ministry that challenge all leaders. First, local churches experience a predictable life cycle of growth and decline. Undoubtedly times of growth are more exciting than times of decline, yet anyone who has worked in a church for very long has experienced both ups and downs. Second, the size of a church impacts its health and vitality. Larger churches are not just bigger versions of smaller ones but entirely different types of organisms. As churches grow bigger, they become more complex with multiple ministries, staff, and services. You cannot lead a large church in the same way you would a smaller one. Third, what got your church to where it is will not get it to where you want it to be! As a church ages and changes size, it demands new approaches to leadership, change, programming, training, and presents a host of new challenges that must be faced. Other than its basic beliefs and values, the two major forces that impact a church's growth are its age and its size.

Life Cycle of a Church

Ministry goes through cycles of ups and downs, victory and defeat, joy and sorrow. Success in any worthwhile endeavor is never an ending but just a point in a cycle of winning and losing that continues year after year. Up-and-down cycles are an ongoing part of life and ministry, as the preacher of Ecclesiastes makes clear:

> There is a time for every event under heaven—a time to give birth and a time to die; a time to plant and a time to uproot what is planted. A time to kill and a time to heal; a time to tear down and a time to build up. A time to weep and a time to laugh; a time to mourn and a time to dance. A time to throw stones and a time to gather stones; a time to embrace and a time to shun embracing. A time to search and a time to give up as lost; a time to keep and a time to throw away. A time to tear apart and a time to sew together; a time to be silent and a time to speak. A time to love and a time to hate; a time for war and a time for peace.
>
> Ecclesiastes 3:1–8

A trusted mentor once said to me, "Gary, you've got to make hay while the sun shines." It was his way of telling me that I needed to be aware of the cycles of ministry and to work with the natural cycles rather than against them. For example, one cycle that is evident among churches in the United States is that worship attendance rises gradually from September through Easter and then declines from Easter through August. This predictable cycle is often called the "summer slump" and is a reality found in most communities throughout the country. Church planters work with the cycle by starting churches any time between September and Easter Sunday, but rarely do they start a new church between Easter and August. Local church leaders are wise to begin new ministries in the fall or winter, not starting something new in the summer (unless it is a summer ministry, of course).

However, while there are numerous life cycles that influence the growth of a church, such as the cycle of worship attendance just noted, a local church's own life cycle has the greatest impact on its health and vitality. One of the first people to identify and highlight the life cycle of the church was David O. Moberg.[1] He wrote, "Study of many churches reveals a typical pattern through which they pass as they emerge, grow, decline, and ultimately die. Each recurrent growth cycle of stability, experimentation, and integration may be described as involving five stages."[2] His five stages are incipient organization, formal organization, maximum efficiency, institutional stage, and disintegration. Unfortunately, even though Moberg's study of the life cycle of the church offered many insights helpful to church leaders, his book was not widely read among local church pastors and leaders. The person who popularized the life cycle concept among church leaders was Robert D. Dale in his book *To Dream Again*. Dale modeled his church life cycle on that of the cycle of human development. He discovered nine stages of church life.[3] In order, his stages are dream, beliefs, goals, structure, ministry, nostalgia, questioning, polarization, and dropout.

Moberg, Dale, and, as we will discover in a later chapter, others point out that all organizations and organisms move through predictable stages of birth, growth, maturity, and decline. Chapter 2 introduces and illustrates this classic life cycle model, while chapters 3 through 7 explain the particular patterns and challenges that a church faces at each stage of

> **Success in any worthwhile endeavor is never an ending but just a point in a cycle of winning and losing that continues year after year.**

development in eight different categories: commitment to mission, involvement of laypersons, congregational morale, facilities, programs and organizational structure, attitude toward change, pastor and staff, and worship and attendance. Following chapter 7 is a profile to help you decide where your church is in the congregational life cycle.

Size of a Church

The impact of size on organizations and organisms is recognized in several disciplines. Various researchers in such diverse fields as economics, business management, sociology, biology, and church growth have all acknowledged the impact of size on organizational development. For example, studies in biology speak of "power scaling relationships," which are mathematical determinations of how characteristics change with size in different species. Geoffrey B. West writes:

> . . . metabolic rate increases as the ¾ power of mass. Put simply, the scaling law says that if an organism's mass increases by a factor of 10,000 (four orders of magnitude), its metabolic rate will increase by a factor of only 1,000 (three orders of magnitude). This represents an enormous economy of scale: the bigger the creature, the less energy per pound it requires to stay alive. This increase of efficiency with size—manifested by the scaling exponent ¾, which we say is "sublinear" because it's less than one—permeates biology.[4]

Research in modern management theory also reflects on the significance of size in managing a business. Larry Greiner, professor of management and organization at the University of Southern California's Marshall School of Business, notes, "A company's problems and solutions tend to change markedly as the number of employees and its sales volume increase. Problems of coordination and communication magnify, new functions emerge, levels in the management hierarchy multiply, and jobs become interrelated."[5] Anyone who has been involved in small and large organizations can resonate with Greiner. Communicating with five people is very different from trying to communicate with fifty or five hundred people. Clearly, small is different from large. Size does matter.

No one in the church growth field has addressed the issues related to congregational size as widely as Lyle E. Schaller. In *The Pastor and the People* Schaller differentiated his advice on the basis of small, medium, and large church categories. In 2000, writing in *The Very Large Church: New Rules for Leaders*, Schaller declares, "Size is the most revealing and useful frame of reference for examining the differences among congregations in American Protestantism."[6]

A number of myths (fallacies) have grown around the subject of church size. For example, one popular perspective speaks of size "barriers"; however, there is little research data to confirm the existence of size barriers. There are some truths (certainties) that have been demonstrated regarding the impact of church size on congregational development. Chapter 10 will review such fallacies and certainties. Chapters 11 through 15 are devoted to a complete overview of how a church's size influences its growth and decline. Each chapter outlines the challenges faced at one of five common church sizes.

Taking It to the Next Level

Continual learning is crucial for any person who wants to get ahead in today's information-rich environment. Recently I saw a sign on the wall of a human resource department that highlighted this truth. It read: "What got you to where you are won't get you to where you want to be." People in almost any field of work see this truth played out annually. They know that what got them their job five years ago is not sufficient to get them their next promotion. If they hope to get ahead, they must take classes to update skills, attend

> **Long-term excellence is always the result of continual improvements over time.**

seminars to network with new clients, or sign up for training to raise their level of expertise.

The same holds true in the sports realm. Every successful sports team learns that the worst part of victory is that it is never final. The strategy that succeeded one year will fail the next. Sports dynasties develop only when members of the team are inspired to improve in a new way year after year. It is what happens in the time off between seasons that makes winners during the season.

It is equally valid that what brought a church to its current level of ministry fruitfulness will not get it to the next level of growth and vitality. Leaders learn quickly that as a church grows and ages, it becomes increasingly difficult to keep it healthy and vibrant. Over time, people change, conflicts build, and programs peak in effectiveness. Long-term excellence is always the result of continual improvements over time.

Cycles of Fruitfulness

This is a book about the cycles of fruitfulness and the importance of continual improvement to diminish destructive forces that keep a congregation from focusing attention on its mission. *Taking Your Church to the Next Level* explains the impact of age and size on churches and outlines the improvements that must be made at each point if a church is to remain fruitful and faithful to its mission over many years.

I have written this book primarily for church leaders, pastors, students (future leaders and pastors), and those who coach church leaders, such as denominational executives and church consultants. It is intended, however, for anyone who cares about the church and desires to see it experience biblical growth. If you have read this far, I have written the book for you . . . and your church.

Use this book as your personal resource manual. Seek out the ideas that fit your current situation and begin using them right away. As you launch into your reading, feel free to jump in at any chapter, particularly if you know your church is at the specific age or size being described. For example, if your church is plateaued between 400 and 800 worshipers, read chapter 13 on the organizational church. If your church is on a downward trend, read chapter 6 that speaks to issues in a declining congregation. Or if your church is five to ten years old, read chapter 3 on the emerging congregation. A quick glance at the table of contents will point you in the right direction. To get the best overall perspective, however, I recommend that you read the book straight through as written. Approaching the book as it is presented offers you a comprehensive understanding of how age and size impact any church.

At the beginning of each chapter, you will find a brief case study—a continuing dialogue among three pastors, Mike, Phil, and Wes. Some readers find this helpful, as it serves to illustrate the concepts presented in the chapter. Other readers may want to move past the dialogue directly into the material. If you don't find the narrative helpful, feel free to skip it and dive right into the rest of the chapter.

Now if you are going to jump around and read different chapters, have fun exploring. But if you are going to read chapter by chapter, move on to chapter 2 to learn about what some church leaders call St. John's Syndrome, or the predictable life cycle that all organizations and organisms experience.

PART ONE

CONGREGATIONAL
LIFE CYCLES

2

St. John's Syndrome

A team can be great for twenty years or more if the leaders can control the destructive forces and refocus the players on their mission.

Pat Riley

"Don't make any rash decisions about leaving your church, Mike." Wes seemed genuinely concerned as he raised his voice slightly above the background music. "Let's talk this through some more."

"No problem," Mike laughed. "I've got all morning to spend with two of my three best friends."

"Oh, really?" Phil seemed a bit perturbed. "Who is your other best friend?"

"I'll never tell," Mike responded with a sense of glee that he had caught Phil off guard.

"Seriously," Wes pressed on. "I think there's something to the fact that New Hope just celebrated its twentieth anniversary. Over the last year, I've been reading about the predictable life cycle that churches tend to travel, and some researchers find the twentieth year of a church is often the beginning of a long-term plateau."

"Sounds like my church," Mike agreed.

"It certainly does," Wes continued. "In fact several things you've mentioned fit right into the typical life cycle model."

"Like what?" Mike probed as he moved to the edge of his chair.

"Well, the fact that New Hope seems to have lost its vision for the future. You said that you and your board have lost a sense of direction. From what I've read, this is a typical problem that first gets noticed around the twentieth year of a church's existence."

"Why is that?" Mike asked.

"Pastors usually come to a church with a vision of what needs to be accomplished. This is particularly true of new church plants, like New Hope twenty years ago. I'll bet if you look back, you'll remember that you and your team had a very clear vision or sense of direction. Right?"

"You're right," Mike agreed. "We all had a strong commitment to building a work for God in our community. We knew our audience and designed plans and strategies to reach them. And even though we knew the exact timing of our growth was in God's hands, we also set goals and had a timetable to accomplish them."

"That's exactly what I mean," Wes said. "Now what appears to happen, according to the life cycle model, is that by the twentieth year a church's original vision and goals have been reached. While this is positive, the leaders of a church begin to experience a sense of loss. Basically, the leaders no longer have a clear sense of direction—they no longer have a vision for the future."

"That sounds like what we're facing at New Hope," Mike acknowledged. "Maybe there really is a predictable life cycle to church ministry."

Yes, Mike is correct. Research has confirmed that there truly is a predictable life cycle that congregations tend to go through. Not just churches but any organization or living organism faces a predictable life cycle. That of all humans can be illustrated using a bell curve.

FIGURE 1
Human Life Cycle

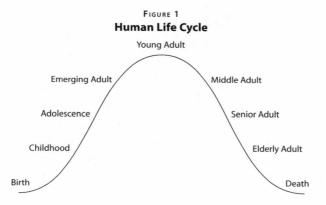

The human life cycle is so predictable that we can attach age categories to each of the designations in the cycle. Childhood is defined as being from a few months to twelve years old. Adolescence comprises the years thirteen to seventeen. Emerging adulthood begins about age eighteen up to thirty, and young adulthood is from thirty-one to fifty years old. What is now being called middle adulthood is between fifty-one and seventy years old, while senior adults are those seventy-one to eighty years old. Elderly adults are people over eighty-one.

The years attached to each life stage designation are somewhat arbitrary. Each person may experience life stages earlier or later than others, or indeed not experience some stages at all due to abnormalities or an early death. Variable factors include a person's family background (genes), lifestyle (for example, smoker or nonsmoker), work (dangerous or safe), and a number of other risk factors that may have an impact on an individual's health and life span. Even though such variables exist, for most of the world's population, the life cycle follows a normal bell curve. We can exercise, eat right, take safety precautions, or practice a number of other preventative measures but we will still go through the life cycle, unless Christ returns during our lifetime.

Job understood the impact of the human life cycle when he declared, "Man, who is born of woman, is short-lived and full of turmoil. Like a flower he comes forth and withers. He also flees like a shadow and does not remain" (Job 14:1–2). The preacher of Ecclesiastes summarizes the human life cycle rather abruptly: "There is a time for every event under heaven—a time to give birth and a time to die" (Eccles. 3:1–2). King David expressed it more graciously, adding a touch of hope when he wrote, "As for man, his days are like grass; as a flower of the field, so he flourishes. When the wind has passed over it, it is no more, and its place acknowledges it no longer. But the lovingkindness of the LORD is from everlasting to everlasting on those who fear Him" (Ps. 103:15–17).

Life Cycle of an Organization

Identifying the existence of a human life cycle leads quite naturally to the recognition that life cycles exist in other spheres of life. The most influential and complex study of the life cycle of an organization has come from Ichak Adizes, who developed a diagnostic theory to describe organizational and cultural change in corporations. His theory was first published as an article in 1979,[1] but most people became aware of his research only after he published *Corporate Lifecycles: How and Why Corporations Grow and Die and What to Do about It* in 1988.[2] In the introduction to his book, Adizes explains: "Organizations have lifecycles just as living organisms do; they go through the normal struggles and difficulties accompanying each stage of the Organizational Lifecycle and are faced with the transitional problems of moving to the next phase of development."[3]

Adizes sees four stages in an organization's growth and four stages in its decline, very much like the human life cycle noted above. He labels the four growth stages courtship, infant, go-go, and adolescence, and the four decline stages he calls aristocracy, early bureaucracy, bureaucracy, and death. In addition to these eight, he adds a ninth stage, called prime, which he feels is ideal. Adizes describes prime as the following:

> In Prime, the organization knows what to do and what not to do. They know when to pass up an opportunity and why to pass on it. The organization has both talent and discipline. It has vision and self-control. It is oriented toward quantity and quality. Both the form and the function are balanced, and they are functional. The organization can grow profitably.[4]

The major challenges of any organization, according to Adizes, are, first, to get to prime, and, second, to stay at or return to prime. It's interesting that in the Adizes model, prime is not the zenith of the bell curve. He calls the top of the curve stable (another stage, making ten stages in all). Prime comes just before stable. Stable, when the life cycle begins to plateau, is actually the beginning of decline when the organization begins to say, "If it ain't broke, don't fix it." Vision, creativity, and innovation are lost during stable, and the organization begins to decline.[5]

One major difference exists between the human life cycle and that of an organization. In the human life cycle, decline is inevitable. No matter how much we exercise, eat healthy food, and visit our doctor, physical decline eventually sets in, leading to death. Paul even acknowledged to Timothy that "Bodily discipline ["exercise" in the KJV] is only of little profit" (1 Tim. 4:8). In the organizational life cycle, decline is not inevitable—only probable. The natural cycle of rise and fall can be reversed, which is good news for those leading any organization in the stage of plateau or decline. Organizations

25

of any kind have the potential for renewed growth and vitality. While the corporate life cycle model speaks primarily to business organizations, it does inform our understanding of a church's life cycle. Fortunately other researchers have applied life cycle thinking directly to local congregations.

The first person to popularize life cycle thinking for churches was David O. Moberg.[6] In *The Church as a Social Institution*, Moberg writes, "As an institution develops, it creates an informal and a formal structure; a set of traditions, values, goals, and objectives; policies and rules; a division of labor; expectations and hopes; collective feelings *(esprit de corps)* and morale among members."[7] According to Moberg, as an organization grows, it moves through phases toward increased institutionalization characterized by increasing bureaucracy, eventually becoming less effective and collapsing under its own weight. "The process by which an institution develops may be called its natural history. Study of many churches reveals a typical pattern through which they pass as they emerge, grow, decline, and ultimately die. Each recurrent growth cycle of stability, experimentation, and integration may be described as involving five stages."[8] Moberg's life cycle model actually focused on how church sects, or new denominations, developed.[9] The five stages he identified were incipient organization, formal organization, maximum efficiency, institutional stage, and disintegration.[10]

Though Moberg was illustrating how larger bodies of churches emerge, grow, and decline, his model was easily adapted to local churches. In 1985 Win Arn, then president of the Institute for American Church Growth, adapted Moberg's life cycle model for local churches in an article, "Is Your Church in a Mid-life Crisis?"[11] Arn kept Moberg's terms for the final four stages but changed the first term to *initial structuring*. Other than that one simple change, the remainder of Moberg's concepts stayed the same, as Arn applied them to local congregations.

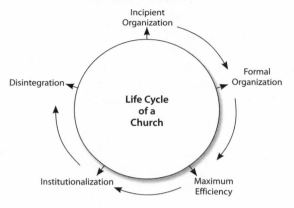

FIGURE 2
Moberg's Life Cycle Model

Using the human life cycle as his primary model, Robert Dale developed an organizational life cycle for churches, which was published in *To Dream Again*.[12] He suggested that there are nine total stages of growth and decline for a congregation: four growth stages, four decline stages, and one plateau stage. Dale called each stage in order from beginning to end: dream, beliefs, goals, structure, ministry, nostalgia, questioning, polarization, and dropout. A glance at his life cycle model shows clearly that it has been adapted from the human life cycle model, and he illustrated it as a bell curve.

Working with the Adizes corporate life cycle model, Martin Saarinen and George W. Bullard Jr. have developed life cycle models that inform congregational growth and decline. In 1986 Saarinen wrote a paper, "The Life Cycle of a Congregation," based on the research of Adizes. First, he presented it at a staff development retreat for a church in North Carolina and later published it as a book with the

Study of many churches reveals a typical pattern through which they pass as they emerge, grow, decline, and ultimately die.

Alban Institute.[13] Saarinen takes Adizes's model, weaves it with the human life cycle model, and introduces what he calls the "Gene Structures of the Congregation." He points out the risk factors for congregations at each stage while creatively adapting Adizes to local churches. George Bullard also builds on the seminal work of Adizes by adding aspects of the human life cycle. He labels the five major phases of a congregation as early growth, late growth, plateau, early aging, and late aging. He changes Adizes's language into that which sounds more appropriate for congregations, using the terms *vision*, *relationship*, *program*, and *management*. Both Saarinen and Bullard borrow largely from Adizes. Each presents fresh ideas, while staying fairly close to Adizes's perspectives.

From Adizes to Saarinen's and Bullard's reworking of Adizes's corporate life cycle model, almost all the work on congregational life cycles has been extrapolated from business models. Some models, such as that of Dale, have been based on the human life cycle, while others, that of Moberg and Arn, are based on sociological studies of denominations and local churches. So the question must be asked, Is there any biblical evidence that a congregational life cycle exists? Clear biblical evidence can be seen for physical life cycles, but what about a congregational life cycle?

The Bible does not address the concept of organizational life cycles directly, but there is at least one illustration of the reality of life cycle movement in local congregations. In Christ's revelation to the church, as found in the biblical book of Revelation, there is a fascinating description of seven churches wrestling with the realities of their life cycle. Each of the seven churches was started slightly before or during Paul's second missionary journey in what is today Turkey, just across the Aegean Sea from Greece. Since Paul's second missionary journey is generally accepted to have occurred between AD 49 and 52, these seven churches were founded either during or slightly earlier than that time. Most likely John wrote the book of Revelation sometime in the early

AD 90s, making the seven churches of the Revelation between forty to fifty years old by the time Christ Jesus addressed them in Revelation 2–3. Given what we know about the life cycle of a congregation, this would put the seven churches toward the end of a long plateau, just before they might be expected to begin a severe decline in ministry effectiveness. This is just what we find.

Christ praises five of the churches for their good qualities (perhaps aspects of their early life cycle) but then he criticizes them for failings (perhaps aspects of their later life cycle). The church in Ephesus had already left its first love (Rev. 2:4). The church of Pergamum was harboring false teachers (v. 14). The church of Thyatira was allowing a wicked and morally dangerous prophetess to influence the believers (v. 20). The church of Sardis looked good on the outside (it had made a name for itself) but was spiritually dead on the inside (3:1). The church of Laodicea was complacent (vv. 15–16). Though Christ did not directly criticize the other two churches, he warned Smyrna to hold firm under persecution (2:10) and encouraged Philadelphia to take advantage of an open door (3:8). The point is that each of the seven churches was beginning to show evidence of decline, and they were only about forty to fifty years old.

Life Cycle of a Congregation

The seven churches of Revelation demonstrate that a natural congregational life cycle existed during the first century. It is not just a modern or postmodern phenomenon but an actuality that has an impact on churches simply because churches are organisms with lives of their own. The life cycle that has been identified in the seven churches of Revelation is sometimes called St. John's Syndrome. A syndrome is a condition that affects organizations or organisms widely enough to be viewed as a normal occurrence. To be labeled a syndrome, a condition must have patterns and characteristics that are identifiable, as well as ones that show up on a predictable schedule or time frame. Such patterns and characteristics are identifiable in local churches, and they will be outlined in detail in chapters 3 through 7. At this point, however, it will be helpful to take a larger view of the normal life cycle of a congregation.

> **Congregations tend to traverse a predictable life cycle that is similar to a bell curve.**

Congregations tend to traverse a predictable life cycle that is similar to a bell curve. A church is prone to rapid growth in the first fifteen to twenty years of its existence, followed by a leveling off of growth onto a plateau for another twenty to forty years. Then follows a slower decline over the next thirty to forty years until the church either closes its doors (dies) or eases into an unhealthy period of stagnation (see figure below).

FIGURE 3

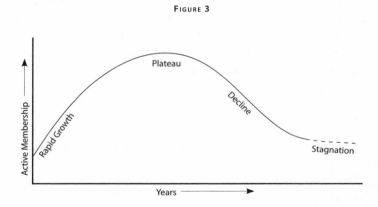

I have seen this picture endless times when working as a consultant with churches. A classic bell curve life cycle is apparent in church A below (a real church but not identified to protect the church's privacy). It was started in the early 1900s and grew rapidly to become one of North America's first megachurches, peaking with a high attendance of 4,250 between 1965 and 1970. During the first twenty years of the church's life, it experienced rapid growth of 318.3 percent each decade (DGR = decadal growth rate), or 15 percent growth each year (AAGR = average annual growth rate). The growth rate occurred even with a slight decline during the second ten-year period. Growth continued but slowed during the next twenty years to 41.4 percent DGR and only 4 percent AAGR (still respectable growth but clearly slowing down). Once the church was past its fortieth birthday, it began to plateau with a very low 1.4% DGR and essentially zero AAGR between its fortieth and sixtieth years. Then, as the graph demonstrates, during the twenty years between the church's sixtieth and eightieth years of existence, it suffered severe decline of -71.1 percent DGR and -12 percent AAGR. As the church nears its one-hundredth birthday, it continues to minister, but its future vitality is uncertain. No church will exactly fit the classic church life cycle, but one can easily see evidence of the bell curve in this church (see figure below).

FIGURE 4
CHURCH A

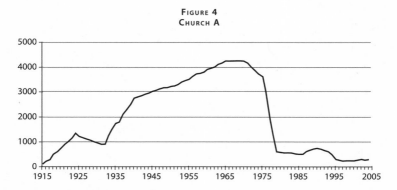

Of course smaller churches go through life cycles also, as is illustrated in church B below. The church was started in 1955 with 16 members and grew rapidly during its first four years to 94, which is a fantastic DGR of 8,266 percent and 54 percent AAGR. Unfortunately, like numerous church plants,

31

church B was unable to sustain its rapid growth momentum and settled into what became a twenty-five-year plateau from 1960 to 1985. During that period the DGR was -3.2 percent with a zero AAGR. Then new life surged into the congregation, propelling it upward again between 1986 and 1988 when it reached a peak attendance of about 265 and then quickly settled down to a second plateau of about 200 people before eventually declining to a low of 55 worshipers by 2008. During the thirty-eighth year of the church's existence, it experienced its greatest growth of 38.6 percent DGR and 3 percent AAGR. Yet in the years since, it has sunk into the natural pattern, declining at a rate of -72.6 percent DGR and -12 percent AAGR. Once again it is clear that churches do not fit the bell curve exactly. All churches demonstrate distinct differences, but one can see the bell curve in the life of church B.

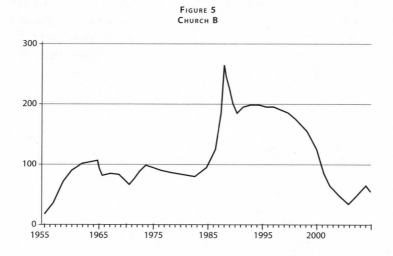

FIGURE 5
CHURCH B

What We Know about the Life Cycle of a Church

Studies of denominations and local congregations have revealed several natural principles that seem to govern a church's progress along the life cycle.

1. All churches are inclined to follow a basic pattern of growth, plateau, and decline. Some travel along the life cycle faster or slower. Others defy the classic pattern for a time, but eventually all churches follow the basic pattern.

2. A church usually grows or declines from stage to stage; that is, it is rare for a church to skip a phase. Thus when a church is in a growth phase, it will tend to go through the stages of growth in their natural order. And when a church is in a decline, it will tend to go through the stages of decline in their normal order.

3. A church's growth and decline do not progress steadily from stage to stage. Movement from one phase to another is often interrupted, with the church plateaued for a period of time before it continues on.

4. The longer a church is plateaued at one stage of growth, the more difficult it becomes to move to the next stage. Growth can be aborted at any stage and decline set in.

5. In some extremely dynamic situations, it is possible for a church to grow so rapidly that the stages are compressed to the point that the church blows right by them, sort of like a jet airplane flying over a crowd at a parade. By the time you see the jet, it is already gone.

6. Normally, churches that remain vital for long periods of time experience not one single life cycle but several life cycles of growth, plateau, and decline.

7. Churches can experience renewal at any point in their life cycle. However, the older a church becomes and the later in the life cycle renewal is attempted, the more difficult it is to see true resurgence of growth and vitality.

So what makes a church durable over the long haul? Why do some churches seem to keep going while others fall into decline? In short, a church's durability comes, first, from the values that guide the creation of its program and ministry;

second, from the development of processes designed to encourage the behavior that reflects those values; and third, from leaders who function as architects of the entire process. The following chapters investigate specific details for each of five stages in the life cycle of a church. I call these stages emerging, growing, consolidating, declining, and dying.

What's Happening?

1. In what ways have you seen life cycles at work in your life, your career, and your church?
2. Can you think of any biblical examples of life cycles?
3. Where would you place your church on the life cycle chart found on page 30? Why would you put it there?

3

The Emerging Church

Behold the turtle: he only makes progress when he sticks his neck out.

James Bryant Conant

Mike stared out the window of the coffee shop, clearly thinking about the conversation, then he said, "I remember the excitement my church planting team felt when we first talked about starting a new church. As we dreamed about what the church might look like, the Lord sort of melted our hearts together."

"I've never started a church," Phil commented. "Tell me more about that time."

"Well, thinking back to those days, the one thing that comes to mind is how scared we all were. We honestly didn't know if we'd succeed or not. We just believed God had called us to start a new church and worked toward that goal with a bit of uncertainty." Mike's eyes brightened up as he spoke. "Our morale was high. Every member of our team had a positive, expectant attitude. We were dependent on each other and we were all willing to work hard."

"What did you do to get ready for your first worship service?" Phil asked.

"Actually it took one whole year to plan our initial worship service. We set a date for our opening service, then worked backward each month laying out a plan of where we needed to be by that time."

"No way!" Phil broke in. "I thought you just rented a building, sent out advertising, and began a worship service."

"No, it takes more planning than that to get a church started. I divided our team into five groups," Mike recalled. "One group focused on the worship service, another on the child care, the third on attracting people to our new church, the fourth on connecting our guests to the church, and the last on administrative details. Each team worked toward the first public worship service so that each aspect would be ready on opening day."

"It sounds like you were very organized," Wes said.

"In a sense we were," Mike nodded, "but in another way of thinking we weren't. We had minimal organizational structure, and our decision making was very spontaneous. We tried several new ministries, and when one didn't work, we canceled it and tried something else. No one seemed to care if we canceled a new ministry. They accepted our leadership and joined in helping make the church a place of effective ministry."

"Whoa, I'd never get away with canceling programs in my church," Phil said. "We've got so many sacred cows I can't change anything."

"That's why I decided to plant a church in the first place," Mike recalled. "I wanted the freedom to try new ministries without having to battle city hall, if you know what I mean."

"So what happened when you finally came to opening day?" Wes quizzed.

"Even though we'd been planning for one entire year, we still had a great sense of uncertainty. We knew the real catalyst was the Holy Spirit, but fifteen minutes before our first public worship service started, I peeked into the auditorium of the elementary school we had rented to see how many people were in the audience. There were only seventeen people there! My first thought was, *This is going to be a disaster*, but by the time the service started, over two hundred people were in the auditorium! From then on out, it's been quite a ride."

The *emerging stage*[1] of a church is unusually challenging and exciting, as a dream for a new church is conceived, nurtured, birthed, and stabilized. Technically this stage lasts around five years, beginning with the new church's first public worship service (see figure below). There are actually three phases in the emerging stage: conception, survival, and stabilization. Conception is the time before the first public worship service when a church planting team is drawn together and plans are laid out for the new church. Conception culminates in the birth of the new congregation when the first public worship service is held. Survival begins at birth and continues through the second year of existence. This is the most dangerous period of the new church's life, as it often operates with limited resources. Stabilization takes place in

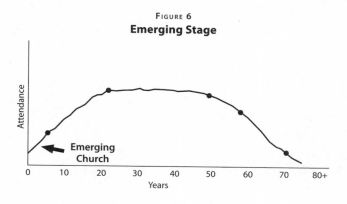

FIGURE 6
Emerging Stage

the next two to five years as the church meets the challenges that arise and begins to realize that it is going to make it into the foreseeable future. Generally a church that makes it to its fifth birthday is stable enough to live for many years. It is out of the emerging, immature phase and can move to the next level.

Characteristics

One of the features of any life cycle is the predictable characteristics observed at each stage. For example, we know from the human life cycle that children have different characteristics than teenagers, and teenagers are different from older adults. The same holds true for the different stages of the congregational life cycle. Churches at the emerging stage are quite different from those at the declining stage, for example. Some of the predictable characteristics of churches in the emerging stage are described in the following paragraphs.

At this stage the mission and vision of the church are clear. Mission is a church's understanding of the biblical reason it exists, while vision is an understanding of how the new church is going to fulfill some aspect of the mission in the community where the church will be planted. Churches in the emerging stage are very clear about what God has called their church to be and do. Sometimes the mission is birthed out of a sense of unrest and dissatisfaction with existing churches, while other times it is from a desire to try a new approach to ministry. In other situations, vision arises from a desire to start a new work for God where none exists. Rarely, however, will a new church survive without a central driving mission and a vision that empower the church and its leaders to move into the future. Together the mission and vision become the fuel that drives the church forward.

During the emerging phase, the founding pastor is the key player whose main role is communicating the new church's mission and casting a vision of a great future for the church that others are able to own. When the founding pastor is able to paint a picture of what the future church might look like in such an attractive manner that others are drawn to it, an atmosphere of high commitment is created that attracts support. Positive attitudes prevail, and people look to the future with hope. The uncertain future demands a visionary leader with enormously high commitment and faith to guide the church; otherwise the church may not survive the first few months or years. Bivocational or subsidized financially, the founding pastor is often a charismatic, prophetic, or apostolic leader who likes to be involved in doing ministry.

> **Rarely will a new church survive without a central driving mission and a vision that empower the church and its leaders to move into the future.**

Another characteristic of the emerging church is the high commitment of early attendees. As the identity of the church is formed, a high degree of collective excitement is created, sometimes seen in emotional and spontaneous worship experiences. However, in churches that emerge from backgrounds where formal or quiet approaches to worship are the norm, morale may be more difficult to pinpoint. High levels of activity and involvement are often a sign of people's commitment to the church. People who participate in the early years of a congregation are normally passionate about spiritual living and particularly excited about how the new church meets their specific needs.

The use of rented or leased facilities is another characteristic of emerging churches. New churches rarely own the space where they meet. Meetings other than for worship are conducted in small groups, which meet as needed in the homes of the founding members. However, people dream of someday owning their own building and acreage to expand their ministry. Often their office space is rented in a high-traffic area of town to give the church a measure of visibility and permanence.

Little organizational structure exists, and trial and error is common as the leaders spontaneously start and close ministries. The new church lives with constant change. Indeed the only constant is change, but change is quickly accomplished and owned by all. Very little opposition to change is noticeable, although a few people may be concerned, especially those with previous church experience.

Emphasis is placed on providing a style of worship that communicates well to non-Christians. In the majority of situations, worship attendance begins with few attendees and then increases over the first year. However, some emerging churches are able to attract large crowds of two hundred or more worshipers from the opening day forward. A great deal depends on the vision of the church, the available resources, and the church's location.

> **The key question that the church seeks to answer in the emerging stage is *Who are we?***

At the emerging church everyone is welcome, and there are many more attendees than formal members of the church. Due to the limited resources, programming is minimal, with most ministries typically aimed at children and their parents. The key question that the church seeks to answer in the emerging stage is *Who are we?* Self-esteem is being formed, and successes and failures in the early years of the church's existence are crucial for establishing and maintaining a positive identity for the church.

Challenges

The characteristics of emerging churches are largely positive. However, churches at this stage of life also face predictable challenges.

Churches in the emerging stage of their life cycle must develop and cast a vision that attracts and holds the number of people and the resources necessary to build a church. To be sure, all emerging churches do not operate equally well from a defined mission or vision. In fact some new churches do very well by simply being obedient to the Great Commission. The Great Commission, found in Matthew 28:18–20 and other places in the Bible, is a solid statement of the church's mission. On the other hand, a vision tells more directly how a church will fulfill the Great Commission in a particular community or region. Smaller churches can do very well operating out of obedience to the Great Commission, but as a church grows larger, it takes a well-defined vision to keep the momentum going. Actually churches in the emerging phase have one powerful vision, and that is to start a new work for God. Once the church is solidly in place, the vision of starting a work is complete. A new vision must take its place or the church will begin to plateau or decline.

Another challenge for churches in the first stage of the life cycle is to develop a viable ministry approach that can be delivered through an "indigenous" worship service and other programs. Since new churches have little if any support base in the form of a congregation, it is crucial that they find a way to connect quickly with their non-Christian community. To do so means designing what missionaries call indigenous ministries and communication. In short, a church must find a way to speak to the very people it wants to reach in such a way that the people hear and respond. This is the reason church planters normally begin with a small, select target audience.

It is impractical for a start-up church to attempt to do too many ministries or programs. It does not have the resources to cut a wide path of ministry impact and thus finds it more fruitful to cut a narrow path that targets a particular audience. During the initial phase of a church's life cycle, it is best to design ministry that is more like a rifle than a shotgun. While a shotgun cuts a wide path, the rifle is more precise. If a church is not able to develop ministries and communication that are understood by its target audience, it is unlikely that the church will experience any significant ministry impact in its early years. In truth the church may actually be stillborn—it may not make it past the first two years.

Related to both of these challenges is the developing of an adequate attendance, or critical mass. Generally speaking, church worship services may be divided into four categories: uncomfortably empty, comfortably empty, comfortably full, and uncomfortably full. When the seating capacity of a church worship service is filled less than 35 percent, a church is uncomfortably empty. This causes a sense of embarrassment to new guests, as they feel too visible to the other people in the audience. When a church's worship attendance fills the seating between 35 to 50 percent, guests feel comfortable. While the auditorium may be somewhat empty at 35 to 50 percent capacity, it is comfortably empty. People don't feel conspicuous. When 50 to 80 percent of the seating is filled, a church is comfortably full. More than 80 percent full and a church becomes uncomfortably full, because when a person enters the auditorium, he or she may have a hard time finding a seat.

The issue for churches in the first stage of their life cycle is to establish enough critical mass that the worship service is at least comfortably empty. Church planters discover they need a minimum of 50 people in the audience for a church worship service to have a dynamic feel that is attractive to newcomers. If an emerging church finds it cannot attract at least 50 people to worship services, the mass is critically low. Churches with fewer than 50 people find it nearly impossible to survive beyond the first two years. Some do, of course, but with fewer than 50 people in the congregation, a church is so anemic that it has little strength to carry on a viable ministry that effectively makes disciples. Such a church is always on the verge of collapse, not having adequate people or financial resources.

Attracting enough financial resources to meet the demands of the early start-up, allowing it to stay alive for the first two to five years, is a related challenge for churches in this first stage. Initial start-up costs include salary for the founding pastor, fees for rental of facilities, money for advertising, incorporation costs, and a host of small items that arise as any new organization gets up and running. Today the trend is for denominations to provide a small portion of the start-up costs, expecting the founding pastor to raise the majority of the initial finances. Fund-raising is a key concern of any new church. If the church specifically targets the unchurched, which most new churches do, it takes a few years to teach the new converts principles of financial stewardship and to see the principles integrated into their lives.

Continuing to develop and modify the ministry model to fit the audience the church is seeking to reach with the gospel is another challenge. Even though a founding pastor and planting team do the necessary groundwork, there is the need to tweak the various programs and ministries. Once an idea for a new ministry is implemented, there are always changes that need to be made. Often it takes from a few months to a couple of years to find an outreach mix that is effective in reaching and keeping new people in the church.

Navigating the transitions from conception to birth to stability is critical for the ultimate survival of the new congregation. What begins with meetings in homes, eventually moves to services in rented facilities, perhaps many different rented facilities. It takes skill to navigate the challenges of such moves. There are leases to be negotiated, moving crews to mobilize, sound systems to set up and tear down—every week! The church must incorporate as a nonprofit entity in the state where it resides. Sometimes members of the planting team will abruptly quit, leaving the founding pastor scrambling for replacements while struggling with feelings of remorse in the loss of beloved team members. These and other transitions must be navigated so the church does not flounder along the way.

The leadership must also develop healthy patterns of discipleship that effectively reach new people for Christ, connect them to the emerging church body, and train them in their spiritual walk and service. Patterns that are established in the first two to five years will often remain with a church for its lifetime. Whatever approach is chosen becomes the *de facto* tradition later on. So putting into place patterns that are fruitful in the beginning stage of a church's life is crucial for its long-term health and vitality.

If the church does not develop or meet the challenges of this stage, it may die an early death (close) or continue on in an anemic manner with little strength. The early stage of a church's life cycle establishes its DNA for the future, and it is as difficult to change a church's DNA as it is that of an individual. Remember, the church is a body, and as a body its DNA becomes its natural way of doing ministry.

What's Happening?

1. Have you participated in a new church plant? If so, what do you remember about the first five years of that experience? During this stage of its life, how was the church different from the church you are in now?
2. What characteristics found in the emerging church do you see in your present church? Which ones are missing?
3. In what way is your church struggling with some of the same challenges that emerging churches face?

	Emerging Church
Mission and Purpose	• Mission very clear • People passionate to fulfill the mission • Energy driving the church into the future
Involvement of People	• People committed • High involvement levels • Mutual dependency • Members willing to work • 50 percent or more serving
Morale	• High morale • Congregational self-esteem being established • Positive attitudes • Hope for the future of the church
Facilities	• Rented or leased facilities • Many meetings held in homes • Dream of having own facility in the future
Programs and Structure	• New programs easily started and canceled • Bare-bones organization • Lots of trial and error • Spontaneity in decision making.
Attitude toward Change	• Change is the only constant • Change viewed as positive • Changes quickly owned by all
Pastor and Staff	• Visionary leader • A "doer" of ministry • Small volunteer staff • Characterized as prophetic or apostolic
Worship and Attendance	• Small but growing • Desire for more people • Designed with the non-Christian in mind
Key Question	• Who are we?

45

4

The Growing Church

It's not where you are today that counts. It's where you are headed.

Arthur F. Lenehan

"When we reached our fifth birthday," Mike continued his story, "we had a big celebration. Since we didn't have a building of our own, we rented the auditorium of the local high school. More than five hundred people filled the seats. The enthusiasm was unreal. Several people who had come to faith at New Hope shared their stories. We asked everyone to stand who had committed or renewed their commitment to Christ while at our church, and more than half of those in attendance stood."

"Wow!" Phil exclaimed. "I wish I could've participated in that celebration. We've never had anything like it at my church."

"I have to admit it was great," Mike confirmed. "But after the celebration was over, our leadership team had a letdown."

"Experiencing a letdown following a celebration is normal," Wes advised. "It's similar to the letdown all pastors face on Monday morning. Sunday is such a big event in the life of a pastor that the lower energy level experienced the day after is a downer."

"True, true," Mike agreed. "That was part of it, but in another sense we knew things had to change. We needed to get out of our rented facility. New ministries had to be started to meet some of the needs of our growing body. Fortunately the first five years had gone so well our morale and momentum were very strong. Our people were open to change and about any new ministry we started."

"I'd like to have some of those problems," Phil commented, looking somewhat discouraged. "Those were problems created by your growth, while the problems at my church are ones created by decline."

"Yes, I guess if you're going to have problems, it's better to have ones caused by growth than decline," Mike agreed, "but they were challenging to us at the time. Fortunately our leadership team made some good choices. To help with our worship attendance, we added additional worship services. This was a good answer until we were able to purchase ten acres of land and build our first units. I guess the biggest challenge was where to invest our resources."

The first ten to twenty years of a church's existence are quite often the best years in terms of its numerical growth. Indeed there is a tendency in churches to take from twenty to twenty-five years to reach their maximum size.[1] While the first five years get an emerging church established, it is the next fifteen years when most of the growth tends to take place. In fact for most churches the largest worship attendance occurs between the fifteenth and twentieth years of their life cycle (see figure below). The following characteristics are typically found in churches during the *growing stage* of their life cycle.

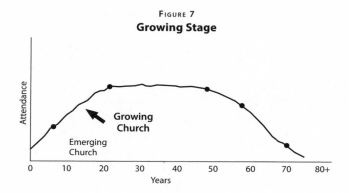

FIGURE 7
Growing Stage

Characteristics

The success experienced in the first five years of ministry leads most churches to even higher levels of goal ownership among worshipers. The strong sense of mission and vision builds as people grow in their excitement about what God is doing in their midst.

Volunteers are easily recruited, trained, and placed in ministry, since everyone wants to be part of the ministry success. Members and attendees alike donate their time, talent, and treasure to empower further development of the church's ministry. When new people come, they are quickly put to work, in part because of the huge need for workers to staff the large number of new ministries.

The call for financial support to purchase the first property and build the church's initial facilities is received well. More money is pledged during the fund-raising phase than is needed. Congregational self-esteem rises as the church successfully completes its first building campaign and construction project. Indeed members dream of building even larger facilities to further expand the church's outreach.

Worshipers are very regular in their attendance and they invite friends and family to come with them. Often the church schedules multiple worship services and childcare to handle the growing attendance. Overall morale continues to build as the number of people attending grows. Core values remain strong, which allows everyone to adopt and accept change.

As new needs are discovered, fresh ministry approaches are implemented to meet them. New programs focus on responding to the hurts of people. Little thought is given to how things may be done in other churches, but signs of future traditions begin to form. During the first five years of life, the church focused mostly on ministry to families with small children. As the church moves on, new programs are added for middle school and high school students. Teamwork is a hallmark of the church during this stage of the ministry, and programs are designed with an outward focus.

> **The first ten to twenty years of a church's existence are quite often the best years in terms of numerical growth.**

The pastor continues to set a strong example by working hard in visible ways, but he is also viewed as a good organizer for the way ministry is integrated. Whenever the church has a workday, the pastor is there serving alongside the members. People sense the need for additional personnel, which results in the hiring of office and associate staff. The pastor delegates effectively some ministry work to volunteers, and a big part of the pastor's role is the development of resources and management systems to meet the demands of growth. All leaders are results oriented and have a concern for the growth of the church.

As more and more new people attend, it becomes evident that more formal ways of keeping the church unified around a common vision and values are necessary. Participants are asked to indicate their commitment to the church by joining or accepting the leaders' authority. Goals are formalized and publicized in an effort to get everyone on the same page. A creed, slogan, or doctrinal statement is established to preserve

The key question faced by churches in this stage of their life cycle is *Where should we invest our resources?*

and propagate the particular positions of the church. Occasionally codes of behavior are instituted to increase the in-group feelings, as well as to distinguish the church's identity from other churches in the community.

The key question faced by churches in this stage of their life cycle is *Where should we invest our resources?* The excitement created by the growth of the church stimulates people to invest in the ministry financially. The early fruitfulness of the ministry offers many options. Deciding which option to fund is a key challenge during this time. Other challenges must be faced as well.

Challenges

Growth creates challenges that, when handled well, propel the congregation farther along the life cycle. New management systems must be designed and implemented to meet the demands of growth. Finances have to be dealt with more professionally, and processes for welcoming and networking new people into the church ministry must be put in place or newcomers will begin to be lost to the overall ministry. Financially the church is stretched, even though people give well. The need for additional staff and facilities becomes a huge issue that must be resourced for the church to continue growing.

New ministries must be started to meet the needs that newcomers to the church bring. As the church grows, the number of need-oriented people will reach critical mass, and the church will need to relate to them. For example, when the church is smaller, there may be only one family with an autistic child. As the church gets larger, more families will have autistic children and enough critical mass develops to have a new ministry geared to this particular need. Or as the church gets larger, a network may form of people who are interested in off-road biking or missions or any number of different needs and concerns. The church must continue to maintain its ministry to the original target group, while adding new ministries to expand and enlarge its reach to other groups of people in the community.

The congregation will press the leaders to develop higher quality ministry as well. In the first five years, when most programs were started, members accepted the low quality of the start-up conditions. However, as time goes by, people begin to expect higher levels of quality in programming, teaching, facilities, music, and just about every aspect of the church's ministry.

Expansion of facilities is another challenge for a growing church. The church will need to purchase its first facilities or, in some cases, rent or lease additional space to keep its growth going. One of the major mistakes in the emerging stage is the purchase of property and a facility that are too small. If the church continues to grow, there will be a need to enlarge existing facilities or relocate to new ones. Related to the size of the facility is the need to use current facilities multiple times.

A clear pathway to leadership is still another challenge for the growing church. Growing people create growing churches. If a church cannot design and put into place a process of leadership development, growth will soon overwhelm the current leaders to the point that they burn out.

It is important for a church to continue to keep its cash flow current; otherwise the ministry may begin to plateau due to a loss of needed financial support. This problem may develop as new staff, ministries, and facilities are added. Wise management of financial resources will be crucial to continued growth. When it is determined that certain ministries or other areas that drain the church of cash do not provide a return for the expenditures, they should be eliminated.

If the worship attendance stays under 150 people for the first five years, church leaders will discover that the informal, relational fellowship so cherished by the founding members will actually hold the church back from further growth. For around 80 percent of all churches, breaking the proverbial 200 barrier becomes a significant issue during this second stage of church life. Long-term worshipers may leave the church because the close feel of fellowship is lost as the church grows beyond 150 to 200 people.

As more new people attend and are connected to the church, competing agendas between the original members (pioneers) and new members (homesteaders) may derail the church's growth. Newcomers may not be aware of the original mission, vision, and values of the church. Old-timers may not feel new people appreciate the sacrifices they made to get the church going. Often the founders of the church have an entrepreneurial spirit, while those who come later seek an already established ministry program. The difference in expectations may create two different congregations competing for the future vision and resources of the church.

What's Happening?

1. What characteristics of a growing church do you find in your own church?
2. Which of the challenges facing growing churches can you identify as issues in your church?
3. Is your church in the growing stage of its life cycle? How do you know?

	Emerging Church	Growing Church
Mission and Purpose	• Mission very clear • People passionate to fulfill the mission • Energy driving the church into the future	• Strong sense of mission and vision • High level of goal ownership • Excited about what God is doing

	Emerging Church	Growing Church
Involvement of People	• People committed • High involvement levels • Mutual dependency • Members willing to work • 50 percent or more serving	• Volunteers easily located • People donate their time, talent, and treasure • New people quickly involved—40 percent serving
Morale	• High morale • Congregational self-esteem being established • Positive attitudes • Hope for the future of the church	• Morale continues to build • Corporate esteem affected by successes and failures • Core values strong
Facilities	• Rented or leased facilities • Many meetings held in homes • Dream of having own facility in the future	• First building units completed • Vision for more property and facilities
Programs and Structure	• New programs easily started and canceled • Bare-bones organization • Lots of trial and error • Spontaneity in decision making	• Function of ministry determines the form • Programs developed in response to needs • Traditions begin to form
Attitude toward Change	• Change is the only constant • Change viewed as positive • Changes quickly owned by all	• Changes easily adopted and integrated • Changes determined by mission and vision • Changes accepted by all
Pastor and Staff	• Visionary leader • A "doer" of ministry • Small volunteer staff • Characterized as prophetic or apostolic	• Full-time pastor with secretary • Sets example as worker • Delegates to volunteers
Worship and Attendance	• Small but growing • Desire for more people • Designed with the non-Christian in mind	• May need multiple services • People very regular in attendance • People invite and bring friends and family
Key Question	• Who are we?	• Where should we invest our resources?

5

The Consolidating Church

There is surely nothing quite so useless as doing with great efficiency what should not be done at all.

Peter Drucker

Mike, Wes, and Phil stopped their conversation briefly to get refills on their coffee. When they returned to the table, Mike broke the silence: "So, that's my story, and I'm sticking with it." He laughed. "After twenty years we're basically stuck, and I don't know where to go next."

"My church has been on a plateau for nearly twenty years," Wes took hold of the conversation. "We haven't grown or declined much, so let me share some thoughts."

"Sure, go ahead," Mike said. "I'm very interested in what you've experienced, since you've been down this road before me."

Wes began: "I've noticed that my church has gradually shifted from an outside focus to an inside focus. Essentially, over the last few decades we've moved from an interest in evangelism to being more involved in spiritual formation."

"But isn't that what a church is all about?" Phil quizzed with a look of surprise.

"Yes, it is," Wes quickly agreed, "but not at the expense of evangelism. A holistic view of discipleship must include reaching out to those who have yet to believe on Christ. As we grew during the first two decades, people slowly began to focus more on the people we already had in the church, while they became less concerned with those outside the church. We started focusing on the refinement of our programs and ministries, rather than starting new ones. We hired a pastor of management and another of pastoral care to do a better job with the resources and people already in the church."

"To echo Phil a bit, isn't that just natural?" Mike asked.

"Sure it is, but that's the problem," Wes added. "What's natural eventually turns inward to bring stability, but then the church becomes so stable that no one wants to grow anymore. People begin to guard the structure and programs already in place, so it is difficult to close out an older ministry, let alone start a new one."

"What about the church's vision?" Phil asked. "I've heard that churches often lose their sense of mission. Is that what you discovered?"

Wes paused, gazing down at the floor, then sighed. "Yes, we slowly lost our sense of the future. Our church was growing up, and we took steps to optimize our ministry effectiveness. Looking at it now, I'd say we tried to make things more efficient but we really didn't replace our old vision with a new one. Once we started focusing on caring for the people and programs we already had in place, we slowly lost our vision for fruitfulness, at least fruitfulness in outreach. For the last twenty years or so, we've been holding on, but I sense that our ministry is slowly losing momentum. One of these days we're going to start declining. I can just feel it coming."

Churches that enter the third stage—the *consolidating stage*—of the congregational life cycle are usually quite healthy. The first twenty years of ministry sparks growth that brings in new believers, as well as those who wish for more energy in their spiritual lives. Over time, however, people become tired of the continual challenges growth brings and begin to desire a stabilized ministry. Leaders sense it is time to leave the youthful stage of the church and move on to consolidate what they have, with consolidation being defined as a stage of calmness as current ministries mature.

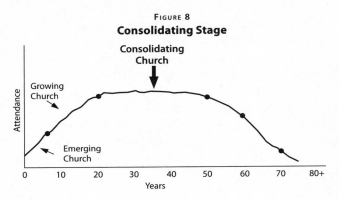

FIGURE 8
Consolidating Stage

Characteristics

The mission and purpose of the church remain strong as a church enters the third stage of its life cycle, but changes are in the air. Leaders appear relaxed, with a clear vision for the church's future. Those who were part of the church at the beginning are now entering their mid-life years. The twenty-something pastor is now more than fifty years old, and the thrills and challenges of the first years of ministry are now tiring. Second-generation members and newcomers are less aware of the mission of the church and not quite as passionate about their own spirituality.

A complete lay-mobilization system is now in place, and a higher quality of leader is being sought out. Everything is done with a measure of excellence. Enthusiasm for serving is beginning to wane, but it is not obvious to most leaders.

Morale is high and is as good as it is ever going to get. Leaders and attendees are confident they can do about anything they wish, due to the years of past success. Everyone is appropriately proud of the church and its track record, maintained for the last two decades. Around town everyone says this church is the one to attend, particularly if you want a church that knows where it is going in the future.

Church facilities are all completed and look up to date. However, the property is maxed out, and leaders are beginning to wonder what to do about it. Some wish to relocate to a new piece of property, while others feel it would be best to plant a daughter church or turn the focus from local church growth to international missions.

> An institution's membership withers when the kind of religious experience the original founders had ceases to exist in the present members.
> —Herb Miller

The essential programs are now formalized. Ministry is maximized but it is more difficult to start anything new. Before starting any new ministry, a proposal must be approved by a committee. During this phase, the formal structure of the church develops rapidly, as commissions, committees, boards, and pastoral staff are appointed and hired to meet the needs of the large congregation.

New ideas, of course, are given serious consideration, but leaders are beginning to be more concerned for efficiency than for fruitfulness. After leaders grant approval for a new ministry, the responsibility for making it happen is delegated to others, and about 30 percent of the people are involved in some form of ministry service. Resistance to change in the way of closing or starting new ministries begins to build.

If the church has grown numerically in the first two decades, the pastor will be overseeing a multiple staff. While the pastor is available to members, especially those from the early years of ministry, most of his time is given to working with board members, staff, and other church leaders. The pastor is self-satisfied with achievements and may write a book or conduct "How I did it" seminars. When the founding pastor retires or leaves for a new ministry, the church calls a new pastor who is more rational and less charismatic. Quite often the new pastor is a gifted manager who can help the church maintain efficiently its well-designed ministry.

Worship services are full, and the church may be using multiple sites or venues to allow for increased attendance. If early worship services were characterized as emotional, church members have now become more sedate as worship leaders plan services that are more acceptable to those who are coming from less emotive backgrounds. Often, due to the overcrowded conditions, newcomers are not noticed, and the number of inactive members increases and they are not missed.

The key question the church seeks to answer is *Where do we go from here?*

People are genuinely proud of what the church has become and overjoyed at finally arriving at what some consider a full-service church. Finances are at an all-time high, and most everyone feels satisfied with the church ministry. Hardly anyone notices that the church is slowly losing its sense of mission and vision, but church leaders begin to ask, *Where do we go from here?*

The third stage of the congregational life cycle can be very short, perhaps ten to twenty years in length, or it can extend to as many as thirty or forty years. The length of the plateau depends on the ability of leaders to sustain the momentum from the first two decades of ministry, as well as on the community and economic conditions surrounding the church context. If a church continues in the consolidating stage for thirty to forty years, it slowly loses momentum, as the sense of mission and vision is lost. The church becomes passive—

reactive rather than proactive—as emphasis is placed on sustaining the institutional gains of the past years.

Fresh approaches to ministry are not allowed, even though there is a feeling that the old programs are not working as well as they once did. Finances remain strong as the founders and early members of the church are now in their best earning years. On the surface all is well and no one senses a need to change. The fastest growing segment in the church is the seniors, and some notice that fewer children and youth are represented in worship services.

Challenges

The major challenge facing churches in the consolidation stage is to renew their mission and vision. The difficulty, of course, is that the entire church ministry is going so well that no one senses a need to change anything. An "if it isn't broke, don't fix it" mentality permeates every aspect of church ministry.

There is great danger at this point. Speaking of this stage in the congregational life cycle, one pastor said, "The saddest day in the life of a church is when it burns the mortgage papers." This pastor was referring to the loss of vision. For twenty-five years church leaders look forward to paying off the mortgage on the church buildings. Without their realizing it, the desire to eliminate debt becomes the vision of the church. When the church makes the last payment, its vision is accomplished. Unfortunately most churches never replace the old vision with a new one. Without a vision, the church enters into a time of slow decline, but no one even remotely notices it at the time. Envisioning a new direction for the church is a must at this stage if the church is to maintain its momentum into the future. Lead pastors must learn to keep the current ministry going while at the same time building a new dream for the future.

Related directly to this first challenge is the increasing need to educate newcomers and second-generation members regarding the mission, vision, and values of the church. Studies show that second-generation believers are not as passionate about their faith or church as their first-generation parents. People who assemble to start a church are drawn together by a common vision to accomplish a great work for God. Planting a church takes faith and a willingness to risk that are not commonly found later among the children of the founding members.

> Don't let your old goals become your tombstone!

Second-generation believers grow up in a church that is already established. They experience fully developed programs and do not know what it is like to struggle. Their parents may be so engaged in the mission, vision, and values of the church that they simply assume their children own them also. Such is not the case, however. What was new, vibrant, and exciting to the parents is old, worn, and out-of-date to the children.

Churches entering the consolidation stage of their life cycle must communicate to the new generation the core values, mission, and vision of the church, and these must be communicated to newcomers as well. People who join a church in the third decade of its existence do not have the same understanding of its basic purposes as those who came earlier. To assume new people will simply "catch" the vision like one would catch a cold is a sure sign of a future slowing of momentum.

> Churches entering the consolidation stage of their life cycle must communicate to the new generation the core values, mission, and vision of the church.

A third challenge is to keep starting new programs and ministries. Once a church enters the consolidation stage, there is a desire to do just that—consolidate ministry. The struggle to provide a full-service ministry that takes place during the first two decades is wearing on the original members. By the third decade many are ready to rejoice and enjoy the full program that the church has in place. They do not understand that new people bring different needs and desires.

Programs are always begun with some need in mind—the program or ministry is put in place because some person or group of persons senses a need and works to meet it. By the time a church enters the consolidating stage, its ministry programs are twenty to thirty years old. While basic needs do not change—the presence of children always means a need for childcare—the way the ministries are designed, communicated, and delivered changes. New needs arise that were not considered in earlier years. For example, half a century ago few churches offered a divorce care program but today almost all do. The basic principle is new ministries reach new people. If a church stops developing new programs, eventually it will stop attracting new people, particularly younger people and their families.

In the first years of a church's life, everyone is quickly involved in serving. Usually new churches are short on workers, so anyone who desires to work is kept busy. Leaders and workers are not always the most talented, but their key talent is availability. Over the following decades, expectations for leaders rise. As the church grows, a larger group from which to select leaders is available. This is a good news–bad news situation. It is good to have leaders with better credentials, but it is bad in that more and more people are unable to find a place of service in the church. Slowly the ranks of inactive people grow as the church puts in place stricter qualifications for those who would be leaders and workers.

Another challenge facing churches in the consolidating stage is to establish processes for assimilating newcomers,

New ministries reach new people.

developing leaders, recruiting workers, and teaching disciples. This is particularly true for large churches. Churches with worship attendances under 200 may be able to welcome, involve, and train newcomers quite easily. The smaller attendance enables leaders to know who is a new person and to provide the personal touch required to engage him or her in the church's ministry. In a larger congregation it's not as easy to spot guests, so churches must develop intentional processes to connect with newcomers. It takes mundane methods to involve new people in the church's ministry. Without well-designed ways to assimilate, recruit, and engage newcomers, many will simply be lost to years of inactivity.

When churches experience significant numerical growth in the first two stages of the life cycle, they will need a larger pastoral team in the consolidating stage. Calling or hiring additional pastors and support staff becomes crucial. Organizing and aligning a staff that works well together as a team is a major challenge, especially for leaders with little team experience. Decisions regarding how paid staff work with volunteers and which ministry programs each will be involved in become important.

Relocating or enlarging the current facility may be another challenge at this stage of development. One of the leading causes of plateauing is related to the size of the church's facility, parking area, and grounds. Decisions made regarding property usage are critical at this stage of the life cycle if the church is to continue growing in the consolidating stage.

What's Happening?

1. Is your church in the consolidating stage of its life cycle? Are you just entering this phase, at the middle, or toward the end?
2. What characteristics of the consolidating stage described in this chapter do you see working in your church?

3. What challenges are you confronting that are similar to those found in this third stage of the congregational life cycle?

	Emerging Church	Growing Church	Consolidating Church
Mission and Purpose	• Mission very clear • People passionate to fulfill the mission • Energy driving the church into the future	• Strong sense of mission and vision • High level of goal ownership • Excited about what God is doing	• High visibility of mission • Common purpose in all ministries • Second-generation members and newcomers unaware of mission
Involvement of People	• People committed • High involvement levels • Mutual dependency • Members willing to work • 50 percent or more serving	• Volunteers easily located • People donate their time, talent, and treasure • New people quickly involved—40 percent serving	• Lay mobilization system formalized • Higher quality of leaders desired • Enthusiasm begins to wane—only 30 percent serving
Morale	• High morale • Congregational self-esteem being established • Positive attitudes • Hope for the future of the church	• Morale continues to build • Corporate esteem affected by successes and failures • Core values strong	• Morale at its highest—this is as good as it gets • Confidence that goals can be reached is contagious • People are appropriately proud of their church
Facilities	• Rented or leased facilities • Many meetings held in homes • Dream of having own facility in the future	• First building units completed • Vision for more property and facilities	• Buildings completed • Property maxed out • Possible vision to relocate
Programs and Structure	• New programs easily started and canceled • Bare-bones organization • Lots of trial and error • Spontaneity in decision making	• Function of ministry determines the form • Programs developed in response to needs • Traditions begin to form	• Programs are formalized • Ministry is maximized; maintenance is minimized • New ministries and opportunities for service still being created
Attitude toward Change	• Change is the only constant • Change viewed as positive • Changes quickly owned by all	• Changes easily adopted and integrated • Changes determined by mission and vision • Changes accepted by all	• New ideas given serious consideration • Leaders responsible for approval • People responsible for implementing new ideas

	Emerging Church	Growing Church	Consolidating Church
Pastor and Staff	• Visionary leader • A "doer" of ministry • Small volunteer staff • Characterized as pro-phetic or apostolic	• Full-time pastor with secretary • Sets example as worker • Delegates to volunteers	• Pastor leads a multiple staff • Pastor works primarily with church leaders • Pastor may lead seminars or write book—"How I Did It"
Worship and Attendance	• Small but growing • Desire for more people • Designed with the non-Christian in mind	• May need multiple services • People very regular in attendance • People invite and bring friends and family	• Worship center full • More inactive members but are not missed • Newcomers not con-nected due to over-crowded conditions
Key Question	• Who are we?	• Where should we invest our resources?	• Where do we go from here?

6

The Declining Church

I've been in business thirty-six years; I've learned a lot—and most of it doesn't apply anymore.

Charles Exley

"Phil!" Wes was trying to draw his friend into the conversation. "What do you think about what we've been discussing?"

"It's been helpful, but I think my church is a little further along than either yours or Mike's," Phil replied. "We've been on a slow decline for some time now."

"That's not good but perhaps it's just a time of adjustment for your church before it moves forward again," Mike tried to encourage Phil.

"I wish that were so." Phil seemed disheartened. "But our decline has been going on for so long now that I think it's going to be very difficult to turn things around."

"How so?" Mike asked cautiously.

"My church is concerned more for its survival than for its mission. In fact our ministries are dwindling, resources are drying up, and people are blaming each other for the decline. We've lost any real sense of mission or vision," Phil replied.

"Have you tried to lead your board in establishing a new vision or dream for the future?" Mike asked.

"Yes, I took my board on a planning retreat three years ago, but it was a disaster. After leading a Bible study on the importance of vision, I asked my leaders to dream of what they wanted our church to be in the next ten years, and no one said a word. They could only seem to think about one year out, and even then they kept coming up with the same old ideas. All they could do was suggest we try some of the programs they remember that worked well years ago."

Phil seemed frustrated. "To tell you the truth," he whispered, "I've been considering the possibility of moving on to another church but I've only mentioned it to my wife. I just don't know what to do to stop this decline."

The fourth stage of a church's life cycle is the *declining stage*. The purpose of the church has been forgotten or outlived, and the major focus of the leaders is on keeping the current ministries going. Mission and vision are cloudy, if they exist at all.

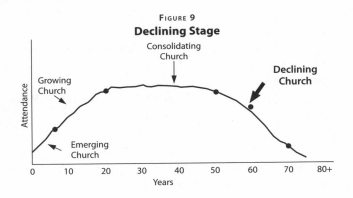

FIGURE 9
Declining Stage

Characteristics

The few newcomers that come to a declining church do not know the vision or mission of the church. Third-generation members seem to have forgotten why their grandparents founded the church. Older members try to restore the former mission and vision of the church to avert decline, but doing so never seems to work as they hope it will.

Newcomers find it extremely difficult to get involved in ministries. Even though they would like to serve, and older members say they have done their part, it's just too difficult to get involved. People assume others will do the work, but no one will, or perhaps can, due to the lack of trust and rigidity. This means that new people are not used until they have been around long enough to be proven doctrinally sound. Unfortunately no newcomers ever stay around long enough to gain the needed trust to be able to serve, let alone become change agents.

Morale polarizes among different groups in the congregation. Some groups are discouraged, while others continue to see some hope for the future. Together the church members have little or no sense of their corporate identity. The older people appear to find their self-esteem by looking back to the glory days when the church was founded. They are nostalgic, sometimes becoming angry when they feel a sense of loss. Most talk revolves around the way things used to be. People despair that the church will ever be vital again, and many become weary from struggles.

The church buildings are beginning to show their age, and deferred maintenance is becoming a problem. There is definitely more space than needed at this time in the church's life cycle. Many feel that the answer to filling the facilities once again is to just work harder, thus they demand more of the pastor, staff, and lay leaders.

Everything is well organized and structured, but it is difficult finding people to serve on the numerous boards, ministries, and committees. The present form of ministry determines its function, and it is nearly impossible to close an existing ministry. Administration is centered in boards, teams, and committees that are self-perpetuating and administration becomes an end in itself as the church becomes a bureaucratic maze. Rather than serving their needs, the church institution becomes the master of its members.

Programs that no longer serve their original purpose are allowed to eat up resources simply because they have always been there. As the many programs use up resources, the real needs among members of the congregation are not met. Since ministry is problem oriented, the stress is on eliminating problems rather than starting new ministries that meet needs. Gradually the quality of ministry declines and disintegrates.

Few changes are proposed, and no changes are considered that depart from the status quo, which someone jokingly notes means, "the mess we are in." Clearly it is the ideas of insiders that are preferred over those of any newcomers, especially those who come from larger churches with strange new ideas on how to do ministry. Original members retire from leadership or service and complain that the younger people or newcomers won't take over and do their part, but at the same time they hope that tomorrow brings back past successes without having to change anything.

The pastor is self-satisfied with past achievements and focuses primarily on the management of the existing program. While overseeing a declining staff, the pastor hopes that the church will experience a quick turnaround involving little pain but knows such a thing rarely if ever happens in real life. As everyone looks for someone or something to blame for the church's decline, some criticize the pastor's lack of leadership, and confidence in the pastor's ability to turn the church around diminishes. Some people share openly their belief that a new or younger pastor is needed. To gain a measure of pride, the pastor serves on a committee for the denomination, joins the local Kiwanis Club, or works long hours with the neighborhood redevelopment agency.

Worship attendance is declining. A few visitors attend worship but rarely return for a second visit. Members no longer feel the worship service is of high enough quality for them to bring family and friends. The worship service is out of touch with the younger generations, and some notice that when high school students graduate, they begin attending a different church in town. Even older members are increasingly absent from worship, with close to 55 percent of formal members coming only two or three times each year. Worship may become so ritualistic in this stage that it is merely a formality to most worshipers. Creeds or doctrinal statements become relics of the past with little meaning for the present challenges being faced by the church or its worshipers.

> **The key question the church seeks to answer is** *How do we stop the decline?*

The question on everyone's mind is *How do we stop the decline?* Unfortunately no one seems to know the right answer or is willing to take the risk to suggest what needs to be done to turn the church in a different direction. The formal bureaucracy dominates leaders, and they are more concerned with perpetuating their own interests than in maintaining the distinction that brought the church into existence and empowered its ministry for so many years. Finances decline, and more and more special offerings are taken as leaders challenge members to give sacrificially.

Challenges

Churches in the declining stage find that problems mount, resources dwindle, ministries decline, and people begin blaming each other for the sad state of affairs. At least five specific challenges must be faced having to do with morale, resources, the blame game, facing reality, and the mission and vision of the church.

A major challenge is keeping hope alive and morale up. Corporate discouragement will lead the church into further decline, so a way must be found to lift up the congregational spirit. The pastor and other church leaders must work overtime encouraging people to trust the Lord, as well as refocusing attention on the mission of the church.

Realigning limited resources is another important task. Closing ministries that no longer make an impact for the good of the church is a difficult step but it must be done so that resources of money and volunteers can be aligned with programs that serve a purpose rather than a tradition. People who serve in nonproductive areas must be reassigned to places of service that produce results. Out of necessity the budget must be trimmed, and money must be carefully and strategically spent on facilities, materials, and programming that will benefit the growth of the church.

Controlling the blame game, as well as the conflict that potentially can arise, is another key challenge for leaders. If leaders are to maintain a level of trust among the congregation, good communication regarding the actual state of affairs is a must. Leaders must be available and open to talk with any and all members and they should encourage people to pray for the church. Instead of blaming others, people must be encouraged to look at the church with realistic eyes and make the hard decisions that will help turn the church around.

> **The future of a declining church depends on the level of pain the leaders are willing to endure.**

Another important step is helping people be honest about the current state of affairs and the future of the church. Often those who are in the midst of a decline overlook the reality of their situation. The job of leaders is to assist the congregation to see reality.

Restoring a sense of mission and vision for the future is a crucial challenge that must be accomplished if the church has any chance of survival. Calling the congregation back to the mission of the church and developing a new vision for the future is essential.

In doing all of this, pastors and leaders must be willing to suffer pain for canceling programs and diverting finances to new projects and ministries. To some extent the future of a declining church depends on the level of pain the leaders are willing to endure. Closing beloved programs, realigning financial resources, and establishing new directions will each garner criticism. Eventually some people may leave the church, but if the church has any chance of being restored to a healthy state, leaders must be willing to endure the pain of the criticisms and abandonment.

What's Happening?

1. Is your church in the declining stage? Why or why not?
2. What characteristics of a declining church do you see in your church?
3. What challenges are you encountering that are typical of churches in this stage of the life cycle?

	Emerging Church	Growing Church	Consolidating Church	Declining Church
Mission and Purpose	• Mission very clear • People passionate to fulfill the mission • Energy driving the church into the future	• Strong sense of mission and vision • High level of goal ownership • Excited about what God is doing	• High visibility of mission • Common purpose in all ministries • Second-generation members and newcomers unaware of mission	• Newcomers and third-generation members do not know the mission • Older members try to restore former mission to avert decline

71

	Emerging Church	Growing Church	Consolidating Church	Declining Church
Involvement of People	• People committed • High involvement levels • Mutual dependency • Members willing to work • 50 percent or more serving	• Volunteers easily located • People donate their time, talent, and treasure • New people quickly involved—40 percent serving	• Lay mobilization system formalized • Higher quality of leaders desired • Enthusiasm begins to wane—30 percent serving	• Original people say, "We have done our part" • Newcomers find it hard to get involved • Some expect others will do work—only 20 percent serving
Morale	• High morale • Congregational self-esteem being established • Positive attitudes • Hope for the future of the church	• Morale continues to build • Corporate esteem affected by successes and failures • Core values strong	• Morale at its highest—this is as good as it gets • Confidence that goals can be reached is contagious • People are appropriately proud of their church	• People lose a sense of corporate identity • Corporate self-esteem is based on looking back to better days • Morale polarizes
Facilities	• Rented or leased facilities • Many meetings held in homes • Dream of having own facility in the future	• First building units completed • Vision for more property and facilities	• Buildings completed • Property maxed out • Possible vision to relocate	• Buildings show their age • Deferred maintenance becomes a problem • More space than needed • Space for meetings not a problem
Programs and Structure	• New programs easily started and canceled • Bare-bones organization • Lots of trial and error • Spontaneity in decision making	• Function of ministry determines the form • Programs developed in response to needs • Traditions begin to form	• Programs are formalized • Ministry is maximized; maintenance is minimized • New ministries and opportunities for service still being created	• Few new ministries added • Forms of ministries determine function • Programs create needs rather than meet needs

	Emerging Church	Growing Church	Consolidating Church	Declining Church
Attitude toward Change	• Change is the only constant • Change viewed as positive • Changes quickly owned by all	• Changes easily adopted and integrated • Changes determined by mission and vision • Changes accepted by all	• New ideas given serious consideration • Leaders responsible for approval • People responsible for implementing new ideas	• Few changes proposed • No change considered that departs from the status quo • Insiders' ideas preferred over newcomers' ideas
Pastor and Staff	• Visionary leader • A "doer" of ministry • Small volunteer staff • Characterized as prophetic or apostolic	• Full-time pastor with secretary • Sets example as worker • Delegates to volunteers	• Pastor leads a multiple staff • Pastor works primarily with church leaders • Pastor may lead seminars or write a book—"How I Did It"	• Pastor focuses primarily on management • Oversees a dwindling staff • Self-satisfied with achievements
Worship and Attendance	• Small but growing • Desire for more people • Designed with the non-Christian in mind	• May need multiple services • People very regular in attendance • People invite and bring friends and family	• Worship center full • More inactive members but are not missed • Newcomers not connected due to overcrowded conditions	• Worship style out of touch with younger generations • 55 percent of members not at worship • Few newcomers attend
Key Question	• Who are we?	• Where should we invest our resources?	• Where do we go from here?	• How do we stop the decline?

7

The Dying Church

When you're through changing, you're through.

Bruce Barton

"I'm afraid my church may be dying," Phil said in a near whisper. "We've been declining for so long that I wonder if there is any hope for us."

"I'm sure this will sound like a cliché," Mike responded, "but with God all things are possible, right? He's a God of miracles, even able to raise the dead."

"Sure, that's right," Phil quickly agreed, "but even though God can raise the dead, he rarely does it."

"What makes you feel so strongly that your church might be dying?" Wes asked.

"Well, for starters all my people seem to care about is meeting the budget. If we can do that each year and meet the missionary budget too, everyone seems to be happy. There is little thought to what God wants to do through our church where we live."

"I didn't realize things were so difficult at your church, Phil," Mike said. "Do you have anyone in your church to encourage you? Anyone to work with you?"

"There are three people that I meet with weekly for prayer. When we're together, we do encourage each other. Unfortunately most of the congregation despairs about the future. We've had to cancel some programs lately for lack of support. For example, we had planned a special outreach event about a month ago, but then we had to cancel it because no one was willing to watch some of the children in the nursery for just two hours. Then again, two weeks ago, I suggested to the leaders that we should advertise our Easter service, and my chairman said, 'We tried that before and it didn't work.'"

"Ugh!" Wes groaned. "I've heard that comment so many times that it makes me sick."

"Me too," Phil agreed. "You know last week we had to let my secretary go because we just don't have the funds for the position any longer. To tell you the truth, I'm seriously thinking it's time for me to leave . . . maybe look for another church."

"I understand why you might feel that way, Phil," Wes spoke up quickly. "But why don't you hang in there a while longer? Mike and I can pray with you and perhaps we can offer some ideas to help bring your church back to health."

"That would be great," Phil said thankfully. "I really don't have much hope but I'm not sure it's time to leave either."

The final stage in the life cycle of a church is the *dying stage*. No one likes to think about churches dying or closing their doors of ministry, but it does happen to about three thousand churches each year.

Characteristics

By the time a church enters the last stage of its life cycle, its sense of mission and vision is almost totally lost. If churches

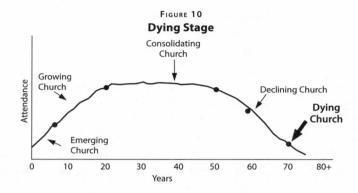

FIGURE 10
Dying Stage

in this stage were honest, they would have to admit that their essential purpose is simple survival.

Ministries that were very fruitful in bygone years are now being eliminated due to a lack of leaders, participation, or funding. Few volunteers are available, as hardly anyone wants to serve in a decaying program. Most people say quietly, "It's the pastor's job. After all, isn't that why we pay him?" Ten percent of the people are doing about 90 percent of the ministry.

Frustration and despair are evident throughout the church. Corporate esteem is based on meeting the budget and missionary obligations. Frustration is very high and morale is extremely low. People feel there is little to no hope for the future. Boredom and passivity are paramount. Disillusionment is a common feeling among the people. Quite often the congregation just gives up and slowly runs out of resources.

During this stage, upkeep of the facilities becomes a critical problem. The church has much more space than it needs, and people actually long for less space and property. It is difficult to get people to help care for the building and grounds. In some cases, when buildings have been allowed to decay, it is a sign that a church is in the last stage of its life cycle. Sometimes, because of a sense of history, the church maintains its buildings at the expense of doing ministry. Then programs and ministries are canceled for lack of support. A few programs are maintained out of respect for tradition but they have little relevance to the real needs of the people.

Often in a dying church, change is perceived as a threat to the church's existence, and people seem unwilling to try anything new. They say, "We've never done it that way before," or "We've tried that before and it didn't work." There is low tolerance for anything new. Members are unwilling to risk failure, as that would cause even greater discouragement. A minority of people control the church by grabbing at the little power they have rather than dying to self so their church might live.

If the pastor is an older person, he may be holding on until retirement. Often a younger pastor will try hard for a year or two to bring about change but eventually will become discouraged and seek a position in another church. People may watch with joy as the younger pastor leaves, saying, "We expected you to leave. Over the years we've trained and sent out many a younger preacher to other churches." In either case churches at this stage normally have part-time pastors serving with meager salaries unless the church operates with an endowment or members have deep financial resources. When seeking a new pastor, people look for someone to save them by a miracle—they hope it will be someone who does not require them to change anything.

The worship center is uncomfortably empty. Newcomers rarely visit and, when they do, most are so uncomfortable, they never return. The music and style of worship are so out of touch with people outside the church that newcomers find it hard to relate. There are more announcements about funerals and people in nursing homes than about new people being baptized or joining the church. Occasionally a worship service will have a large attendance, but normally that would be one that is a homecoming or anniversary celebration.

> **The key question the church seeks to answer is *How can we turn this mess around?***

77

Leaders ask, *How can we turn this mess around?* Unfortunately most are not open to the drastic changes that might bring hope for the future, so they continue to struggle until they are financially unable to keep open the doors of the church. Most of the time, churches die a slow death. However, churches are tough, and as long as sufficient resources are available, the church may live for many years beyond any viable ministry.

Challenges

Churches that find themselves in the last stage of the congregational life cycle are in a very tenuous situation. Death is near, and several challenges are waiting in the near future.

On the hopeful side is the potential of rebirthing the church. The greatest challenge is leading the people to embrace the necessary changes to allow God's Spirit to work anew in the life of the church. It has been observed that when churches have successfully restarted, they do at least the following:

1. They establish a new definition and commitment to mission.
2. They change their attitude so the people and leaders look to the future with hope and excitement.
3. They change their priorities concerning the use of financial resources.
4. The church organization is reworked to allow for faster decision making, new program development, and greater flexibility in all aspects of church life.
5. New resources, materials, and approaches to ministry are embraced. In most situations the church needs the assistance of an outside person to see this happen.

On the less hopeful side of the picture is the need for a church to acknowledge its real situation, allowing the leaders to make difficult choices about when and how to close the ministry. This involves counseling people as they manage their feelings of hurt and loss.

Generally the dying process takes place in three steps:

1. As a result of declining finances, the church is no longer able to secure a full-time pastor.
2. This leads the church to secure the services of a part-time pastor who may be a layperson with independent financial resources, a retired pastor looking for extra income, a young pastor seeking a first ministry experience, or a pastor who is shared with another congregation. In nearly all of these situations, the church ministry dwindles as people leave for other congregations that provide more adequate ministries.
3. The church reaches a point when, financially, it can no longer keep the doors open. The church dies and merges with another congregation, simply goes out of business, or turns over control to the denomination.

> The greatest challenge is leading the church to embrace the necessary changes to allow God's Spirit to work anew in the life of the church.

Generally speaking, a church can exist in the dying stage for many years if the community around the church remains the same and the money holds out. However, when the community context changes and money becomes scarce, it is just a matter of time until the church closes.[1]

Both options—rebirth or death—present challenges to church leadership. The unfortunate truth is that in most cases churches choose to die rather than go through the pain of rebirth. It is easier for church members to close the doors of their beloved church than it is for them to change.

Key Indicators for Church Closure

A decision to close a church should never be made on the basis of any single indicator below, but taken as a whole, these indicators can provide church leaders with helpful insights as to the future potential of a church.

Indicator #1: Public Worship Attendance

A church needs at least fifty adults to have a public worship service that is celebrative and attractive to new people. Having twenty to forty adults at worship puts a church in an unhealthy situation. Less than twenty adults is a strong indication the church should be closed.

Indicator #2: Total Giving Units

It usually takes a minimum of ten to twelve faithful giving units to provide for a full-time pastor. It takes another ten to twelve units to provide for the ministry of a church in terms of supplies, advertising, etc. Thus, a church reaches a danger point when it has twenty-five or less giving units.

Indicator #3: Lay Leadership Pool

As a rule of thumb, a church needs one leader for every ten adult members (junior high and up), one leader for every six elementary children, and one leader for every two children below school age. Less leadership will make it difficult to provide for the needs of a growth ministry.

Indicator #4: An Effective Ministry

A church needs at least one ministry for which it is known in the community. For example, one church may be known for its great Sunday school, another for its children's program, and another for its ministry to senior citizens. Is the church known for a particular ministry?

Indicator #5: Past Growth Rate

A growth rate that has been declining for five to ten years should serve as a warning signal. If a church is only about one-fourth or less of its original size, it is likely to be facing hard times and may face eventual closure.

Indicator #6: Congregation's Spiritual Health

A church's spiritual climate is another factor to be considered. Is the church characterized by peace, happiness, and love? Or is there a spirit of anger, bitterness, and discouragement?

Indicator #7: Average Membership Tenure

How long have people been attending the church? If the average tenure is longer than twenty years, it is a sign that the church is having difficulty reaching and assimilating new people.

Indicator #8: Focus of Church Goals

Is the focus of the church on itself or outward to new people? Do leaders talk about ministry, mission, and purpose? Or do they talk about paying the bills, hanging on, real estate, the past, and membership care?

Indicator #9: Budget Expenditures

Where is the money spent? On outreach, advertising, and ministry? Or are these areas the first to be cut when the budget gets tight?

Indicator #10: Church Rumors

Is there positive talk about God and his work in the church? Are there people who believe God can renew the church in the days ahead? Or do people talk about the past, respond pessimistically to visionary statements, and fail to recognize that God is at work in their church?

Evaluation

If you are faced with a church you think should possibly be closed, the following questionnaire may prove helpful in giving you an objective evaluation.

Circle Yes or No for each question.

1.	Does this church have an average public worship attendance of over 50 adults?	yes	no
2.	Does this church have twenty-five faithful giving units?	yes	no
3.	Does this church have a least one competent lay leader for every ten adults?	yes	no
4.	Does this church have at least one ministry for which it is known in the community?	yes	no
5.	Does this church have a positive growth rate over the past ten years?	yes	no
6.	Does this church demonstrate a healthy spiritual life?	yes	no
7.	Does this church have an average membership tenure of less than twenty years?	yes	no
8.	Does this church talk about its future goals of ministry?	yes	no
9.	Does this church actively spend 5 percent of its budget on outreach to the local community?	yes	no
10.	Does this church have hope that God can renew its growth and vitality?	yes	no

Tally the Yes answers

7–10: excellent—this is a church with great potential.

4–6: fair—this is a church with unclear direction. It may grow or may decline.

1–3: poor—this is a church with a limited future.

What's Happening?

1. Do you think your church is in the dying stage? Why or why not?
2. What characteristics of a dying church that are described in this chapter do you find in your church?
3. Are any of the challenges found in dying churches being confronted in your church? Which ones?

	Emerging Church	Growing Church	Consolidating Church	Declining Church	Dying Church
Mission and Purpose	• Mission very clear • People passionate to fulfill the mission • Energy driving the church into the future	• Strong sense of mission and vision • High level of goal ownership • Excited about what God is doing	• High visibility of mission • Common purpose in all ministries • Second-generation members and newcomers unaware of mission	• Newcomers and third-generation members do not know the mission • Older members try to restore former mission to avert decline	• Sense of mission and purpose is lost • Purpose is meeting the budget and survival
Involvement of People	• People committed • High involvement levels • Mutual dependency • Members willing to work • 50 percent or more serving	• Volunteers easily located • People donate their time, talent, and treasure • New people quickly involved—40 percent serving	• Lay mobilization system formalized • Higher quality of leaders desired • Enthusiasm begins to wane—30 percent serving	• Original people say, "We have done our part" • Newcomers find it hard to get involved • Some expect others will do work—20 percent serving	• Few volunteers available • Ministry programs eliminated due to lack of leaders or participation • People say, "It's the pastor's job" • 10 percent do 90 percent of the work
Morale	• High morale • Congregational self-esteem being established • Positive attitudes • Hope for the future of the church	• Morale continues to build • Corporate esteem affected by successes and failures • Core values strong	• Morale at its highest—this is as good as it gets • Confidence that goals can be reached is contagious • People are appropriately proud of their church	• People lose a sense of corporate identity • Corporate self-esteem is based on looking back to better days • Morale polarizes	• Frustration and despair are evident • Corporate self-esteem is based on meeting the budget and meeting missionary obligations

	Emerging Church	Growing Church	Consolidating Church	Declining Church	Dying Church
Facilities	• Rented or leased facilities • Many meetings held in homes • Dream of having own facility in the future	• First building units completed • Vision for more property and facilities	• Buildings completed • Property maxed out • Possible vision to relocate	• Buildings show their age • Deferred maintenance becomes a problem • More space than needed • Space for meetings not a problem	• Upkeep and maintenance a problem • More space than needed • Desire for less space
Programs and Structure	• New programs easily started and canceled • Bare-bones organization • Lots of trial and error • Spontaneity in decision making	• Function of ministry determines the form • Programs developed in response to needs • Traditions begin to form	• Programs are formalized • Ministry is maximized; maintenance is minimized • New ministries and opportunities for service still being created	• Few new ministries added • Forms of ministries determine function • Programs create needs rather than meet needs	• Programs canceled for lack of support • Maintenance is maximized; ministry is minimized • Tradition drives ministry
Attitude toward Change	• Change is the only constant • Change viewed as positive • Changes quickly owned by all	• Changes easily adopted and integrated • Changes determined by mission and vision • Changes accepted by all	• New ideas given serious consideration • Leaders responsible for approval • People responsible for implementing new ideas	• Few changes proposed • No change considered that departs from the status quo • Insiders' ideas preferred over newcomers' ideas	• Closed to change • People say, "We've never done it that way" • People say, "We tried that before, and it didn't work"
Pastor and Staff	• Visionary leader • A "doer" of ministry • Small volunteer staff • Characterized as prophetic or apostolic	• Full-time pastor with secretary • Sets example as worker • Delegates to volunteers	• Pastor leads a multiple staff • Pastor works primarily with church leaders • Pastor may lead seminars or write a book—"How I Did It"	• Pastor focuses primarily on management • Oversees a dwindling staff • Self-satisfied with achievements	• Pastor looks forward to retirement • Staff eliminated due to budget concerns • Pastor may move to another church with more potential

	Emerging Church	Growing Church	Consolidating Church	Declining Church	Dying Church
Worship and Attendance	• Small but growing • Desire for more people • Designed with the non-Christian in mind	• May need multiple services • People very regular in attendance • People invite and bring friends and family	• Worship center full • More inactive members but they are not missed • Newcomers not connected due to overcrowded conditions	• Worship style out of touch with younger generations • 55 percent of members not at worship • Few newcomers attend	• Worship center uncomfortably empty • 65 percent of members not at worship • Newcomers rarely seen and almost never return
Key Question	• Who are we?	• Where should we invest our resources?	• Where do we go from here?	• How do we stop the decline?	• How can we turn this mess around?

Where Is Your Church in the Congregational Life Cycle?

Given the dynamic quality of church organizations, it is impossible to pinpoint exactly where a church is on its life cycle curve. All churches are in constant movement from one stage to another, and characteristics of more than one stage are often commingled. Answering the following set of questions will assist you in determining *your* church's profile and its place on the life cycle curve. To get an even more accurate assessment, copy this questionnaire and distribute it to as many leaders as possible, then combine their responses to discover what the majority perspective is. Asking some laypersons to complete the survey and then comparing their assessment with that of the leaders might reveal some different and valuable viewpoints.

Life Cycle Questionnaire

To assess the health and vitality of our church, please answer as honestly as possible the following questions. There are no right or wrong answers, so answer to the best of your knowledge.

Please circle only one answer for each question.

Transfer the final total to the chart below.

84

SA = Strongly Agree   A = Agree   U = Uncertain   D = Disagree   SD = Strongly disagree

1. Our church's mission (purpose), vision, and values are clear to everyone who attends.   SA   A   U   D   SD
2. Morale is high at our church.   SA   A   U   D   SD
3. People are excited about what God is doing in our church.   SA   A   U   D   SD
4. It is easy to begin a new ministry at our church.   SA   A   U   D   SD
5. People are bringing their friends and family members to church.   SA   A   U   D   SD
6. Our pastor is a visionary leader, always coming up with new ideas and dreams for the future.   SA   A   U   D   SD
7. We have more people attending worship this year than five years ago.   SA   A   U   D   SD
8. It is easy to find volunteers to serve in our programs.   SA   A   U   D   SD
9. Newcomers become involved quickly in serving our church.   SA   A   U   D   SD
10. People have a positive attitude about the church.   SA   A   U   D   SD
11. Everyone supports our church's goals.   SA   A   U   D   SD
12. There is a sense of mutual dependency among the members, and we work well together.   SA   A   U   D   SD
13. Our church property and facilities are well maintained and up to date.   SA   A   U   D   SD
14. Changes are easily adopted in our church.   SA   A   U   D   SD
15. We have multiple worship services each weekend or are giving serious consideration to doing so.   SA   A   U   D   SD
16. There is a willingness in our church to begin new programs and cancel old ones.   SA   A   U   D   SD
17. Change is the only constant in our church.   SA   A   U   D   SD
18. Our pastor is considered to be a great organizer.   SA   A   U   D   SD
19. We have few traditions in our church.   SA   A   U   D   SD
20. Worship services are designed with the unbeliever in mind.   SA   A   U   D   SD
21. Our people frequently get together outside of worship services, i.e., small groups.   SA   A   U   D   SD
22. At our church we know who we are and where we are going.   SA   A   U   D   SD
23. New ideas for ministry are viewed positively in our church.   SA   A   U   D   SD
24. In the future we hope to multiply our ministry by enlarging facilities or using other sites.   SA   A   U   D   SD
25. The number of pastors and support staff is increasing each year.   SA   A   U   D   SD

Total the number of answers in each column: ___   ___   ___   ___   ___

Multiply each column by: ↓   x2   x3   x4   x5

Answers after multiplying the column: __ + __ + __ + __ + __ =

Add all of the numbers together for a final total of: _____

FIGURE 11

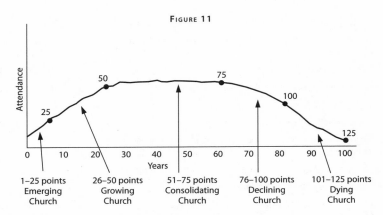

Place an X on the life cycle line that represents approximately where your total from the profile on the previous page would fall.

This profile is a tool to help you analyze where your church falls in its life cycle. Compare the results on this chart with your original estimate in figure 3 found on page 30, and then answer the following questions.

1. How closely does the result here match your earlier estimate?
2. If the two are quite different, what do you think made the difference in the way you originally perceived your church and now?
3. Do you believe the designation for your church, indicated on the above chart, is accurate? Why or why not?
4. What have you discovered about your church?

8

Leading through the Stages

> Leader, you have to be looking out the windshield, not the rearview mirror, to go forward.
>
> James Taylor

"When I was in seminary," Wes remarked in an effort to summarize the morning's conversation, "one of my professors told us never to take a church unless we could envision ourselves staying there a lifetime. That sounded good at the time, but after pastoring for a number of years I see how difficult it is to develop healthy growth through a church's life stages."

"Leading a church throughout its life cycle is really challenging, isn't it?" Phil asked.

"I agree," Mike reflected. "Pastors who are able to lead a church well for thirty to forty years deserve a lot of respect. Just renewing a church's vision every ten or so years is a challenge, let alone fighting off a church's tendency to become focused inwardly."

"Based on our conversation, I think pastors have to change their leadership style at each life cycle stage if they are to have any chance of leading a church for two or three decades," Phil suggested. "Do you agree?"

"You bet!" Mike said, nodding his head. "During the first few years of my church plant, all the people wanted from me was to make something happen. We experimented a lot, and to tell you the truth, the ministry was very unorganized. Then, I think about the fourth or fifth year, things changed. People started complaining about the lack of organization. One person told me that we needed to get our ducks in a row. All of a sudden I realized that I had to be more organized if the ministry was to flourish. I had to change my leadership style."

"In my case," Phil added, "the people aren't concerned about being better organized. They are worried about reviving the ministry. They want me to do something that will bring back the vitality of bygone years. I'd say they just want me to make something happen, much like you did when you first planted New Hope."

"That's true, but there's one difference," Mike offered.

"What's that?" Phil asked.

"You have years of past ministry baggage to deal with, and I didn't have that in a new church plant. To turn your church around, you'll have to be some sort of a superhero."

"Maybe we should start calling you Super Reorganizer," Wes said, laughing.

"Sure," Phil played along. "What type of costume do you think I should wear?"

While the congregational life cycle model is predictable, and most churches tend to follow it, it should not be seen as inevitable. Church leaders can and do interrupt the typical process. Some churches flame out in the early years, never to reach their full potential. Others overcome the predict-able downward drop by continuing to focus resources on outreach even as the church grows older. However, the ten-dency to follow the basic life cycle is strong enough that breaking the pattern requires intentional, sustained, powerful intervention.[1]

While recognizing that no two churches are exactly the same, I believe the five-stage life cycle model presents the most common developmental pattern found in Protestant churches in the United States. All churches are at some point on the life cycle curve. Some stay at one point for shorter or longer periods of time than others. A few blow right through one stage on the way to another. Some do not survive long enough to experience all of the stages. Generally, however, most churches go through at least the first three stages: emerg-ing, growing, and consolidating. If we hope to see churches restored to fruitful ministry, it is crucial to understand the dynamics of the congregational life cycle.

Leadership Observations

Occasionally it is suggested that pastors should not consider accepting a call or appointment to a church unless they can envision staying there the rest of their lives. On the surface this sounds like good advice but in reality it almost never happens. From a practical perspective, recent graduates in all fields, including pastoral ministry, use their first and second jobs to get experience. These initial ministry experiences allow pastors to define their skills, passions, and abilities in ways that study in a classroom never approaches. From a leadership perspective, it takes uncommon ability to adjust one's leadership style to fit the changing needs of a congre-gation as it travels along its life cycle. The bottom line is it takes different skills to lead a church during each stage of its life.

The Catalyzer

During the *emerging stage* of the congregational life cycle, a church looks to the founding pastor to be a *catalyzer* (CAT).[2] A catalytic leader is a person who has the ability to bring something into being that did not formerly exist. In the business world this individual is called an entrepreneur.

FIGURE 12

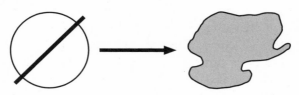

A catalyzer starts a group from scratch, attracting people and resources.

An effective catalyzer evidences three essential skills: vision, communication, and motivation. A catalytic leader is able to define and communicate a clear direction for the church's future. This requires the foresight to see opportunities long before others do. When inevitable obstacles come along, these leaders have the ability to stay focused on achieving the vision and are not easily sidetracked.

> **A catalytic leader is able to define and communicate a clear direction for the church's future.**

Catalytic leaders also have the skill to express ideas in a clear, simple, and direct manner in one-on-one situations or in larger group settings. Equally important is their willingness to listen to others, showing them that their ideas are being valued. Lastly, they motivate themselves and others to fulfill the vision for the future. Personally they stay involved in the process and give the proverbial 110 percent every day.

With a passionate commitment to action, catalytic leaders create success with a fierce can-do attitude. In motivating others they transform their followers from a group of individuals into a highly productive team that understands and supports the vision and has a sense of urgency to get it done. They are also able to develop a strong loyalty and trust among team members. It is not surprising that this type of person is usually found leading a church at the beginning of its life cycle.

Catalyzers may find it difficult to pastor a congregation beyond the first two or three years unless they are able to adjust their leadership style to that of an organizer. Often they become frustrated if they are required to give energy and time to organizing what they have started. If they are unable to recruit a team member to take responsibility for organizing the church, they may move on to start another congregation. True catalyzers are scarce, perhaps numbering only 2–3 percent of all leaders.

The Organizer

In the *growing stage* (stage two) of the congregational life cycle, a church needs the pastor to be an *organizer* (ORG). An organizer has the ability to take a disorderly organization and bring together its jumble of pieces into an orderly form that maximizes its resources.

FIGURE 13

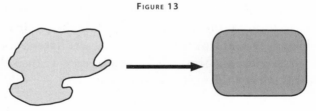

An organizer assembles pieces into an orderly organization that maximizes its resources.

Organizers typically have the skill to develop the internal systems to meet the demands brought on by the church's growth. They design better ways of handling cash flow, involving people in ministry, connecting guests to the fellowship, and managing all resources to maximize the congregation's growth.

Organizers are multitaskers who juggle numerous programs, concerns, and challenges with a well-managed team of assistants. They relish the challenge of bringing order out of chaos. Thus, when the original disorder is finally under control, they may desire a new challenge and move to another church or ministry that needs their organizing skills. Some may be able to morph their leadership style into that of an operator (with the leadership skills needed in the next stage), but most will find advancement in their careers by changing jobs frequently. Organizers are in larger supply than catalyzers, perhaps comprising 10–15 percent of all leaders.

> **Organizers develop the internal systems to meet the demands brought on by the church's growth.**

The Operator

The *consolidating stage* (stage three) requires the skills of an *operator* (OP). An operator likes to manage a stable congregation by making small incremental changes that maintain the basic systems. They care about doing things correctly rather than doing the correct things. On the positive side they bring great unity and calmness to a congregation but they can also become frustrated when faced with disorder or major changes in the philosophy of ministry.

FIGURE 14

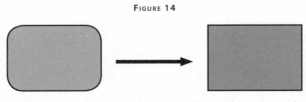

An operator keeps an organization going by improving its general procedures and systems.

92

Operators enjoy times when ministry runs smoothly without any major changes in the structure of the congregation. They feel gratified when things are functioning within predictable boundaries and are not concerned about the church growing, as long as it is running properly.

Reports, meetings, and procedures are a joy to this type of leader. In the worst case, operators may overvalue their role, forgetting what got the church to this stage in the first place. They may even criticize the catalyzers and organizers who came before them, and by doing so force such types to exit the church for other places of ministry. Over time, operators gain control of the church's programs and systems, bringing them under such rigid control that growth slows down (plateaus), leading to the decline and eventual death of the church. It is generally accepted that most church leaders are operators, perhaps numbering around 75 to 80 percent of all leaders.

> **Operators manage stable congregations by making small incremental changes that maintain the basic systems.**

The Reorganizer

When a congregation enters the *declining stage* (stage four), a new type of leader is required if the church is going to experience a turnaround and refocus on the future. When an operator continues in the role of pastor, the church gradually declines until the operator leaves because there is nothing left to operate. To experience renewed growth, the church needs a *reorganizer* (REORG). A reorganizer has skills similar to those of an organizer but with the added ability to work with a congregation in a declining situation.

> **Reorganizers have the skills to keep the long-term members happy while building a new vision and agenda for the future.**

FIGURE 15

A reorganizer brings turnaround strategies to bear on an organization that is in decline.

While organizers work with churches that are growing, reorganizers work with ones that are in the midst of decline. Thus reorganizers have the skills and the charismatic personality to keep the long-term members happy while building a new vision and agenda for the future. They are able to please long-term members and build, simultaneously, a new congregation within the old wineskin. Essentially, they must have exceptional people skills, allowing them to maintain credibility and likability with the established members while reorganizing the church to attract and keep a new constituency.

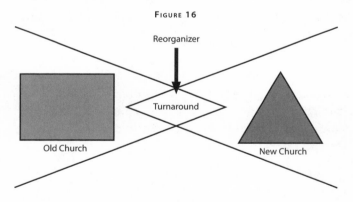

FIGURE 16

Reorganizer

Turnaround

Old Church

New Church

Reorganizers are drawn to a church due to the challenge it presents. They will, however, be prone to leave if the church does not make sufficient headway in a renewed direction within two to three years. Reorganizers are also in short supply, perhaps numbering about 5 percent of all church leaders.

The Super Reorganizer

The final stage of a congregation's life cycle is the *dying stage*. By the time a church reaches this point in its life cycle, it needs what may be labeled a *super reorganizer* (Super-ReOrg). Having the basic skills of an organizer, this person has the added ability to bring radical change that results in the rebirth of a church that is near death.

FIGURE 17

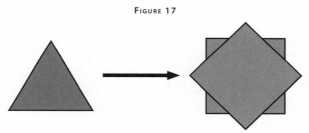

A super reorganizer brings radical changes to a church that result in a total rebirth of the congregation.

Bringing about a rebirth requires desperate measures and most often is accomplished only in a church that is willing to try almost anything to renew its ministry. Super reorganizers are in extremely short supply, perhaps numbering around 1 to 2 percent of all church leaders. Super reorganizers may reorganize only one ministry, although some pastors find they are good at bringing about radical changes in churches that are near closure. Such gifted leaders may find a niche in a denominational role, in the ranks of those providing intentional interim pastorates, or as an outside church consultant. In these positions it is easier to suggest radical changes due to the fact that the super reorganizer's paycheck is not tied to the pleasure of the dying church.

Super reorganizers bring about radical changes that result in the rebirth of the congregation.

Applying this perspective on leadership to the congregational life cycle model offers a new way of predicting the leadership needs of a church at each stage of its development (see figure below).

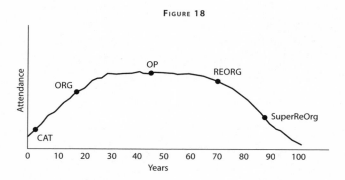

FIGURE 18

As can be seen in the figure, a catalytic style of leadership is appropriate for a church in the emerging stage of the life cycle. An organizer, who pulls together the jumbled pieces of ministry created by the catalyzer, appropriately follows the catalyzer. An operator follows the organizer, bringing congruence to the overall church ministry, but this leader also sows the seeds of eventual decline. Toward the end of the congregational life cycle, a reorganizer is needed to bring about a turnaround. If a radical rebirth is needed because the church is near death, a super reorganizer can do the job.

Turnaround Observations

There are numerous reasons for the tendency of churches to decline after the initial years of growth, but the principal one is the loss of vision for the future. Consider for a moment what takes place in terms of vision during a congregation's move through its life cycle.

Most new churches are started by pastors who are in their youthful years of ministry, mostly their twenties or thirties. Older people do, of course, start churches, but overwhelmingly church planting is a young person's game. The young pastor dreams of establishing a new work for God, to reach a new generation, and eagerly shares ideas, hopes, and dreams with potential team members. Once enough people buy into the pastor's dream, steps are taken to birth the church. Over the next fifteen to twenty-five years, the initial hopes and dreams propel the leaders forward as pieces of the dream begin to fall into place.

Somewhere between the fifteenth and twenty-fifth year, the original pastor and members begin to realize that God has faithfully brought their dream to fruition. By this time the pastor, along with most members of the original team, is in his forties or fifties. After two decades of struggle, they all rejoice in the completion of their vision and settle in to reap the benefits of a mature ministry.

Depending on the power and extent of the original vision, the energy it provides can generally last upwards of twenty to forty years. Seldom do leaders realize that the energy provided by the original vision is beginning to wind down. In fact they may not notice the loss of energy for another couple of decades until the church is forty to fifty years old. Eventually the energy dissipates and the church begins to decline, which is exactly what the congregational life cycle depicts.

Think of a large cruise ship traveling at top speed. What would happen to such a ship if it suddenly shut off its engines while in the middle of an ocean? Would it come to an immediate stop? No, the momentum established would keep the ship going. The passengers would not notice the slowdown at first and would likely keep enjoying the various activities on deck. Very slowly, almost totally unrecognized, the ship would begin to slow down. The friction of the water and waves working against the hull of the ship, while at first hardly perceptible, would create drag, slowing the ship. Winds blowing against the upper decks, again going unnoticed, would push against the ship, adding to the overall resistance. Eventually the ship would come to a stop, drifting aimlessly on the waves and currents.

This is a perfect picture of what takes place in most churches, especially those that have experienced great success. Ministry is going so well that no one notices the loss of momentum as the initial vision is fulfilled. The momentum from the first decades of ministry continues to provide energy for several more years, but at an ever-decreasing rate. The momentum that is created in the emerging stage is realized in the growing stage and institutionalized in the consolidating stage. Church leaders generally discern a problem only when the church enters the declining stage. One of the first signs that people are aware of the slowdown is when they say, "I remember when . . ." By looking back to a former pastor, days of more dynamic programs, or memories of working together when times were challenging, the people signal the current lack of a powerful vision. In effect they look back in an effort to get their corporate self-esteem from the vision of the past.

FIGURE 19

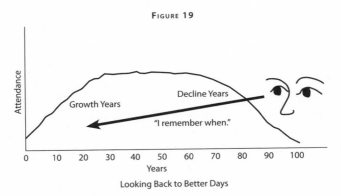

Looking Back to Better Days

Fortunately a church is not condemned to travel a predictable life cycle, and leaders may, and a few do, interrupt the cycle to create new cycles of growth *before* decline sets in. Of course the difficulty is that leaders must introduce a new vision, new priorities, new ministries, new procedures, and a new direction for the church while everything is going well.

The fact that the ministry is at its peak makes it difficult to introduce change exactly because things are going so well.

But it is when the church is doing well that church leaders must develop a new vision and direction for ministry if they wish to avoid the normal pattern of plateau and decline. If they wait too long, the seeds of decline set in, making it increasingly difficult to restore lost momentum (see figure below). A point naturally follows the peak of the growth stage when leaders must decide on the future direction of the church. At this point of transition between stages in the life cycle there is an opportune time for the church to decide to move forward and birth a new cycle of life and vitality or stay on the pathway to plateau and eventual decline and death. These transitional points are *choice points*, when the church makes choices about its future.

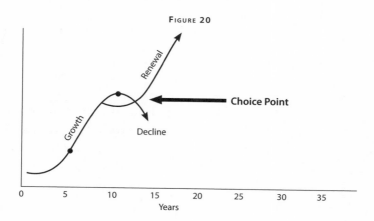

FIGURE 20

Churches that have an effective and fruitful ministry for many years actually go through several cycles of birth, growth, and renewal. At each peak of the growth cycle, the church leaders face another choice point. Leaders who make strategic choices to renew the ministry see continuous renewal; those who do not move strategically most likely see a downturn in the ministry.

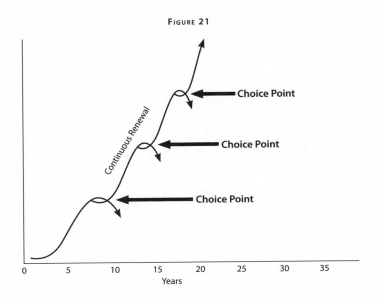

FIGURE 21

Choice Point

Choice Point

Choice Point

Continuous Renewal

Years

Adding this to our life cycle model of leadership, we can see that a church needs a different leadership style at each choice point in the cycle of continuous renewal (see figure 22). At each choice point, leadership must become more catalytic to establish a new vision and sense of direction for the future growth of the church. As the new cycle grows, leaders must become organizers, putting the new pieces together. Eventually leaders become operators for a short time while allowing for catalytic leaders to engage a new vision for the next cycle. As each new cycle is strategically designed, the skills of a reorganizer may also be used to catalyze the new sense of direction.

In some cases a single pastor is able to adjust his leadership style, moving from catalyzer to organizer to operator and back again to fit the church's particular needs. Unfortunately most leaders are not able to freely bounce back and forth between differing styles of leadership, which requires a succession of pastors coming and going at each transition point.

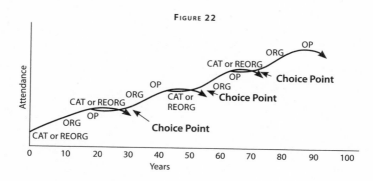

FIGURE 22

What's Happening?

1. Based on where your church is on the congregational life cycle (see figure 11 on page 86, does your church need a CAT, ORG, OP, REORG, or SuperReOrg?
2. How well does the current leadership of your church fit the style that is needed? Consider the senior pastor, other pastoral staff, and lay leaders.
3. Has your church been able to renew its life cycle in the past? If not, why not? If yes, describe what and how it happened.
4. What will it take to renew your church?

9

Growing through the Stages

Our options are to learn this new game . . . or to continue practicing our present skills and become the best players in a game that is no longer being played.

Larry Wilson

"This conversation is very helpful." Wes seemed to express the feelings of Phil and Mike too. "But understanding a church's natural life cycle may be just the surface of the problem."

"What are you getting at?" Phil asked with a somewhat puzzled look.

"Well, a few years ago I started losing some weight. At first my wife and I saw that as a good thing, but gradually I started realizing something was wrong. One day I became ill and had to go to the emergency room. After running some tests, the doctor told me something was going on inside my body but she didn't know exactly what it was. She advised me to see my family doctor. After a series of additional tests, my doctor

102

discovered that I had a kidney stone. My loss of weight was being caused by a problem that was inside of me."

"I see what you're getting at," Mike interjected. "You're saying that a church's life cycle may show just the surface problems that are caused by deeper issues in a church."

"That's right," Wes affirmed. "I wonder what is actually going on beneath the surface of a church that causes it to grow in the first half of its life cycle and decline in the second half. Maybe the things we've been talking about are just surface problems, but what core issues are creating the problems in the first place?"

As we have seen, the congregational life cycle demonstrates two essential patterns that all churches can expect to see—a pattern of growth and a pattern of decline. The pattern of growth lasts from just a few years to perhaps a maximum of fifty years, although for most congregations growth stops between the twentieth and twenty-fifth year. The second pattern lasts for another twenty-five to fifty years, with the church eventually closing its doors sometime between the ninetieth and one-hundredth year.

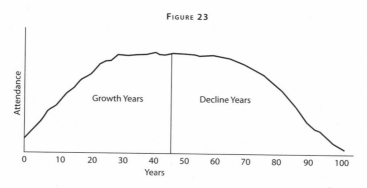

FIGURE 23

Each life cycle has a front side of growth and a back side of decline. Vision is one key aspect related to the front side, as noted in the previous chapter. Another element that influences

103

a church's life cycle is the type and focus of its ministries. The impact of a church's ministry capital is revealed in the intertwining of two feedback loops.[1]

Feedback Loops

All congregations have both positive and negative feedback loops. As people are added to a church, the total congregation grows in size. When church attendance increases, people become confident and proud of their church's ministry. Naturally they reach out to involve their friends and family members in their church, creating a loop that brings in even more people. The main influences on the positive feedback loop are conversions, people transferring in, and births.

FIGURE 24
Positive Feedback Loop

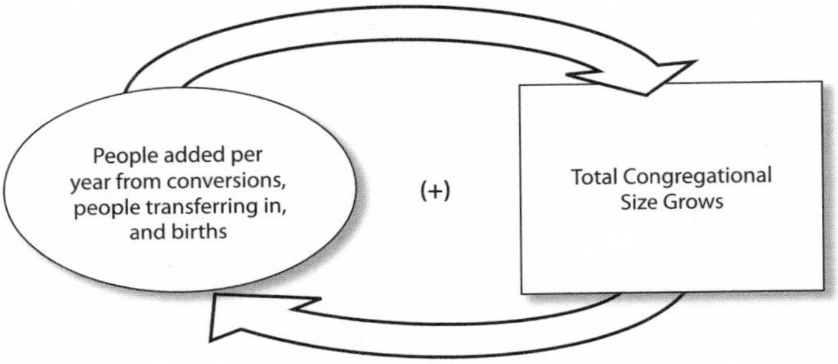

As people are subtracted from a church, the total congregation declines. This action is the exact opposite of the positive feedback loop. As church attendance decreases, people become discouraged and disappointed. The negative corporate self-image that develops among the people causes them to neglect outreach to friends and family. Due to their high level of loyalty to the pastor, their friends, and the church in general, people continue to attend but they lack the necessary pride that would encourage them to reach out to others and invite them in. The main influences on a negative feedback are reversions (people who drop out), people transferring out, and deaths.

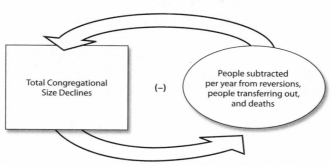

FIGURE 25
Negative Feedback Loop

Total Congregational Size Declines

(–)

People subtracted per year from reversions, people transferring out, and deaths

Each feedback loop is in constant operation with people being added and subtracted from the church on a regular basis. The feedback loops intersect, creating a dynamic feedback loop, resulting in either growth or decline of the church. If the positive feedback loop dominates, then the church grows. When the negative feedback loop dominates, the church declines.

The feedback loops intersect, creating a dynamic feedback loop, resulting in either growth or decline of the church.

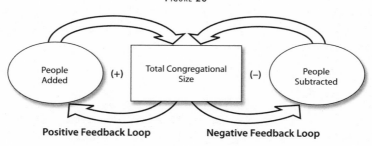

FIGURE 26

People Added

(+)

Total Congregational Size

(–)

People Subtracted

Positive Feedback Loop   **Negative Feedback Loop**

105

Applying the feedback concept to the congregational life cycle model gives another perspective on the reason churches have a propensity to grow in the first part of their life cycle while declining in the second. During the first two stages of a church's life cycle (emerging stage and growing stage), the positive feedback loop dominates; while in the last two stages (declining stage and dying stage), the negative feedback loop dominates. In the consolidating stage there is a tenuous equilibrium between the feedback loops, leaning slightly to the positive side early in the third stage and slowly shifting to the negative as time goes by.

FIGURE 27

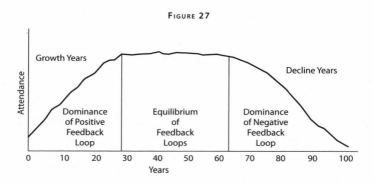

During the consolidating stage, when there is a measure of equilibrium and the positive and negative feedback loops are balanced, leaders may be tempted to try to keep the church at this level. However, observations of many different types of organizations demonstrate three core facts about this stage. First, the state of equilibrium offers a false sense of peace and health. Second, it cannot last for long. Third, it eventually degenerates into decline and collapse.

Ministry Capital

During the first two stages of a church's life cycle, the positive feedback loop is energized because emphasis is placed on mission, vision, evangelism, assimilation of newcomers, and the creation of need-meeting ministries. Contextually appropriate ministries are developed that connect with people, and the structure of the church is fluid and flexible, guided by leaders who are driven by a sense of mission. Relationships are forged in the heat of an expanding ministry. Facilities are in the process of being built to meet the needs of a dynamic growing community of faith. All of this ministry capital is invested in a way that multiplies the church's growth.

Unfortunately ministry capital is not permanent. As facilities age, ministries fail to meet needs, worship increasingly becomes contextually out of touch, leaders cautiously resist change, and long-term relationships are strained, the negative feedback loop is energized, leading to a downward spirit of decline. Now the positive ministry capital that empowered the church to growth in the first two life cycle stages becomes negative capital, dragging the church down in the final two stages (see the two figures that follow).

> **Yesterday's successes become tomorrow's (or today's) problems!**

FIGURE 28

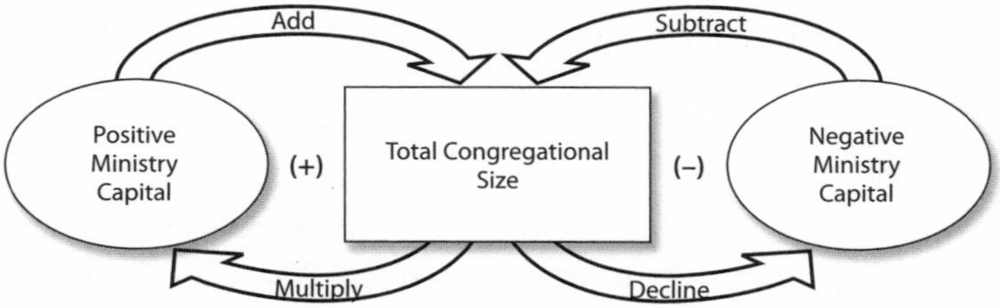

The problem is a church may have had a fruitful ministry in the early stages of its life cycle, but the leaders become attached to the methods, programs, procedures, and general ways of doing things. Yesterday's successes become tomorrow's (or today's) problems! The proclivity of church leaders is to try harder by working more at what they have always done, when, in truth, the need is to find, develop, and use new ministry capital. The old saying is true: *it's best to work smarter not harder.*

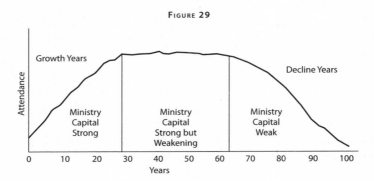

FIGURE 29

Part of working smarter means understanding the impact of ministry capital on the growth and decline of a church. Ministry capital is made up of five core resources: spiritual, directional, relational, structural, and physical.

Spiritual resources relate to the soundness of a church's doctrine, values, and beliefs. The prayer life of the corporate church and its leaders, as well as the faith that everyone has in God's mission and vision for the church, are part of the spiritual resources of the church. Doctrinally sound, praying churches tend to grow better than those that are not.

Directional resources involve the quality and experience of the pastor and the leadership team. Also the commitment of church members to investing their time, talent, and treasure in the church ministry add to this resource.

Relational resources are the unity, fellowship, and community experienced by the corporate body in large, medium, and small groups. For example, churches experiencing conflict tend not to grow as well as those that have loving relationships.

108

Structural resources comprise organizational philosophy and ways of working together. Generally, the more flexible the structure of a church, the greater the potential for growth. The more rigid the structure of a church, the greater the potential for decline.

Physical resources are the value of facilities and property, as well as the visibility and accessibility of the church meeting place. For the most part, a good location adds positive capital.

These five core ingredients come together to form ministry capital, which is an investment in the growth of the church.

FIGURE 30

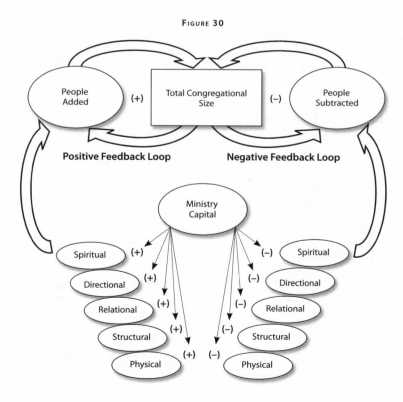

109

Opportunity and Danger

Looking at church growth based on a congregational life cycle model reveals several important clues as to the reasons a church declines in the later stages. First, there is an interconnected feedback system alerting a church to the positive and negative aspects of the church's ministry (see figure 30). Wise church leaders will pay close attention to the feedback received along this interconnected highway. If a church is not growing, it is a clear signal that the ministry capital is losing power, and new capital needs to be discovered, developed, and put into place. If the church is growing, it is a signal that the current investment of ministry capital is paying dividends.

Second, ministry capital activates or deactivates the feedback systems. If the feedback systems are reporting bad news, it is crucial to check the church's investments of ministry capital. Which of the five core areas of capital continue to bring in dividends? Which are reporting losses?

Third, there are certain stages when the church has opportunity to grow but other times when the church is in grave danger of decline. I call these two zones "green" for opportunities and "red" for danger.

FIGURE 31

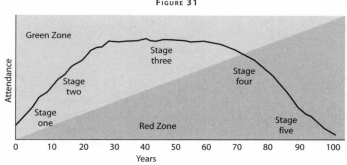

Churches in the first three stages of their life cycle have the greatest opportunity for growth and development. It is

110

during these times that establishing a vision and direction for the church is done with the largest number of resources. Churches in the final two stages are in the gravest danger. During these final stages, resources are limited and momentum is directed downward. But it must be remembered that churches at all stages can be and are being restored to new levels of fruitful ministry.

What's Happening?

1. Which feedback loop is currently dominating your church?
2. What is the state of your ministry capital?

Capital	Strengths	Weaknesses	Opportunities
Spiritual:			
Directional:			
Relational:			
Structural:			
Physical:			

3. Is your church presently in a green zone or a red zone? What does this mean for the future of your church?

PART TWO

CHURCH SIZE
STAGES

10

Step Up to the Next Level

I skate to where the puck is going to be, not where it has been.

Wayne Gretzky

"All this talk about the different phases of a church's life cycle is helpful," Phil pressed on. "But how does a church's size fit into all of this? I mean, isn't there a difference between a church averaging 50 people at worship and one averaging 500?"

"Sure there is," Wes agreed. "My first church had only 54 people. It was easy to communicate to everyone. All I had to do was talk to one or two people and the grapevine did the rest."

Phil laughed. "Yes, and sometimes the grapevine works too well. In my church, word often spreads too fast. I remember when my wife and I discovered we were going to have our third child. We wanted to keep it a secret but, before we knew it, the whole church was aware."

"Yeah! I've been there too," Wes said. "Yet, when I was in my larger church, you know the one with about 500 people, I found it difficult to communicate with everyone in the church. I couldn't rely on the grapevine for the simple reason that it didn't work. Too few people were connected to the grapevine, and when I tried to communicate through such natural networks, word never got out to everyone. I discovered that I had to design a system of emails, phone calls, postcards, and letters to make sure the entire congregation got the message."

"Let me throw this out," Mike said. "I'm back to what we said earlier about size barriers. Size does seem to be important, and I can't help but think from what I've heard that there are certain barriers that churches find difficult to surpass."

"I've heard of the 200 barrier," Phil acknowledged. "But then others, like that speaker we heard, say that size barriers are just a myth."

"I don't know," Wes shot back. "All I know from my experience is that it is difficult to get a church to grow beyond certain levels. In fact my denomination published a report last year that showed 90 percent of our churches are under 100 in average worship attendance. I've never heard of a 100 barrier, but it appears my denomination has one at that level!"

Churches operate differently depending on the size of the congregation. "Right sizing" the various ministries and processes of communicating, welcoming, training, involving, and a host of other activities is crucial for smooth operation, as well as increased growth, of a church. As a church grows, it cannot simply employ business-as-usual practices. Larger churches are not just bigger versions of smaller churches; in reality they are an entirely different entity that requires different operational procedures.

Impact of Size on Organizations

The impact of size on organizations and organisms is recognized in several disciplines. Researchers in such diverse fields as economics, business management, sociology, and missiology have all acknowledged the impact of size on organizational development.

Business Management

Research in modern management theory reflects on the significance of size in managing a business. Larry Greiner, professor of Management and Organization at the University of Southern California's Marshall School of Business, writes, "A company's problems and solutions tend to change markedly as the number of its employees and its sales volume increase. Problems of coordination and communication magnify, new functions emerge, levels in the management hierarchy multiply, and jobs become interrelated."[1] Anyone who has been involved in small and large companies can resonate with Greiner. The ease with which one communicates with five employees is very different from trying to communicate with fifty employees or with five hundred.

Henry Mintzberg, Cleghorn Professor of Management at McGill University, also acknowledges the importance of understanding the impact of organizational size on management practices. "The size of the overall organization appears to have a considerable effect on what senior managers do," writes Mintzberg. "Specifically, we find that chief executives of smaller organizations engage in fewer formal activities but are much more concerned with the operating work of their organization."[2] Mintzberg observes that in business enterprises senior executives of smaller companies tend to focus on operating the organization, internal issues, maintaining workflow, real-time concerns, and informal connections. In contrast, executives of larger companies tend to focus on directing the organization, external issues, maintaining wide perspective, future-time concerns, and formal connections. In a later book Mintzberg suggests three hypotheses concerning the effects of size on organizational structure:

1. The larger the organization, the more elaborate its structure—that is, the more specialized its tasks, the more differentiated its units, and the more developed its administrative component.
2. The larger the organization, the larger the average size of its units.
3. The larger the organization, the more formalized its behavior. [3]

An additional example from the business field comes from Theodore Caplow. Writing in *How to Run Any Organization*, Caplow introduces the concept of "discontinuities of scale."

The diminution of consensus about organization values and goals is a normal consequence of growth, attributable in part to the inherent difficulty of getting a larger number of people who know each other less well to agree about anything, in part to the importation of new people and ideas, but mostly to the brute fact that as an organization grows, its relationships to its members and to the environment necessarily change, so that its original values and goals become somewhat incongruent with its current program. These problems are magnified by discontinuities of scale. An organization cannot grow indefinitely in small increments. Sooner or later it makes a quantum leap that transforms its whole character: the company acquires a second factory in another state; the family has its first child; a summer camp adds a winter program. Often the people involved do not realize that anything significant has occurred until they discover by hard experience that their familiar procedures no longer work and that their familiar routines have been bizarrely transformed. [4]

As organizations grow, Caplow submits, one can expect theft to rise, original members to become obsolete, and an increased dependence on outsiders. He offers five standard methods for coping with organizational growth: team management, decentralization of operations, standardization of procedures, centralization of financial control, and expansion of communication.[5]

Sociology

Early insight on the impact of numbers in social life comes from Georg Simmel (1858–1918). A translation of his work by Kurt H. Wolff, *The Sociology of Georg Simmel*, published in 1950, contains a large section called "Quantitative Aspects of the Group."[6] In this work Simmel acknowledges that larger groups must develop new forms, forms that smaller groups do not need. He comments: "It will immediately be conceded on the basis of everyday experiences, that a group upon reaching a certain size must develop forms and organs which serve its maintenance and promotion, but which a smaller group does not need."[7] Additionally, Simmel recognizes that some groups have sociological structures that make it impossible for them to increase in size. For instance, he mentions "the sects of the Waldenses, Mennonites, and Herrnhuter."[8] The social structure of such groups demands a tight solidarity that cannot be experienced in larger group structure. Simmel notes that the larger an organization becomes, the less inclined it is to radicalism, the more important simple ideas become, and the greater the decrease it experiences in inner cohesion.[9]

One insight Simmel mentions that I have not found in other works is the relationship of absolute and relative numbers. For instance, he asserts that the relative impact of key individuals increases as the group grows, even if the number of key people remains proportionally the same. Thus "it is easier for an army of 100,000 to keep a population of ten million under control than it is for a hundred soldiers to hold a city of [10,000] in check, or for one soldier, a village of 100 . . . in spite of the fact that the numerical ratio remains the same."[10]

Simmel also introduces the concept of the intermediate structure, which is neither small nor large. "The character of the numerically intermediate structure, therefore, can be explained as a mixture of both: so that each of the features of both the small and the large group appears, in the intermediate group, as a fragmentary trait, now emerging, now disappearing or becoming latent."[11] According to Simmel, the intermediate structure shares the essential character of both the smaller and larger structures. The amount of sharing, however, alternates between the smaller and larger characteristics (that is, the intermediate structure moves back and forth between small and large aspects).

David O. Moberg reviews several aspects related directly to church size in *The Church as a Social Institution*. Regarding church conflict, he remarks, "Some evidence indicates that petty jealousies, bickering, back-biting, spites, and personal or factional quarrels are the most prevalent in small congregations which stress intensely emotional types of religious experience."[12] Speaking about people's commitment, he writes, "Increasing size of a church congregation appears to be accompanied by a diminution of the average member's sense of obligation to work, give, and participate."[13] Addressing the importance of evaluation, he reports that one study found four factors of church vitality: youthful vigor, financial giving, increased membership and baptism, and consistent growth. Then he notes that "the larger churches outstripped smaller ones on all four measures."[14]

Another sociologist, Paul E. Mott, addressed the impact of population size on organizational development. In *The Organization of Society* Mott outlines thirteen propositions regarding population size and social structure. In the interest of space, just a sampling of his ideas will be mentioned. Mott attests that as organizations increase arithmetically, "the number of possible channels of interaction increases geometrically."[15] Or, put another way, as the size of a group increases by addition, the number of communication pathways multiplies. Thus the larger the organization, t difficult the communication process. Furthermore organization grows larger, the number of roles increases and they become more formalized. While one leader may be sufficient for small organizations, when organizations become larger, they require more leaders fulfilling more formal, specialized roles. Lastly, Mott states that as the organization enlarges, the authority structures become decentralized, which in turn creates increased levels of influence and rank in the organization.[16]

Sociologist Ronald L. Johnstone builds on Mott's analysis in *Religion and Society in Interaction*. Summarizing Mott's major thesis, Johnstone writes:

> As groups increase in size, the degree of consensus among members concerning goals and especially norms decline. In great part a basic problem of communication and interaction is involved here. As groups grow, a point is reached when not everyone can interact with everyone else; nor can any one person interact with all the others. Levels of understanding and commitment to goals and norms cannot be maintained. Not only can't people share as fully with one another and reach truly common understandings by involving everyone in decision and policy making, but also problems of increasing diversity arise as more members come in. In fact, each new person is a potential disrupter, if not a potential revolutionary, inasmuch as the ideas he brings with him or that he may develop may challenge fundamental tenets of the group. Obviously, the tight-knit, integrated, primary-group-like relationship that may have existed at a group's inception and during its early development begins to submit to increasing diversity and more specialized interests as different elements enter.[17]

Johnstone discusses several additional issues that organizations face as their size increases: declining norms, increasing deviance, development of specialized roles, greater role of

> Church organizations are much more like secular organizations than has been imagined. There is no question that the purpose and objectives of the secular and sacred realms differ significantly, but the people who seek those ends are typical human beings who relate to each other in very similar ways, whether the organizations are sacred or secular.
> —Bill M. Sullivan

autonomy and coordination, and increasing bureaucracy.[18]

Church Growth

No one in the church growth field has addressed the issues related to congregational size as widely as Lyle E. Schaller. As early as 1973 Schaller differentiated his advice on the basis of small, medium, and large church categories. In *The Pastor and the People* he defined a small church as one with fewer than 100 people at worship, a medium church with 100 to 200 worshipers, and a large church with more than 200 worshipers.[19] Two years later he observed in *Hey, That's Our Church!* that churches tend to group at four size levels or plateaus: 30–35, 70–85, 115–135, and 175–200.[20] This appears to have been the first time that the natural gathering of churches around certain size measures was recognized in church growth literature.

In most of his books Schaller discusses the impact of size as almost a side issue. For example, in *Effective Church Planning*, it is within the context of a discussion of small and large groups that he introduces some of the same findings noted by several sociologists. He writes, "In the well-managed small group the internal communication system usually is informal, unstructured, and highly effective. In the large group the internal communication system must be intentional, systematized, structured, and redundant."[21]

Schaller wrote three books in the 1980s specifically targeted to different size churches. The first was *The Multiple Staff and the Larger Church*. This was followed by *The Small Church IS Different*, and *The Middle-Sized Church*. Not only did these three books signal a new approach to church growth (one based on size), but they also communicated new definitions of *small*, *medium*, and *large*. Schaller classified churches into seven size categories: fellowship (35), small (75), middle-sized (140), awkward size (200), large (350), huge (600), and mini-denomination (700).[22] Eventually this classification developed into the following widely used analogy of church sizes.

Average Attendance	Type	Analogy
<35	Fellowship	Cat
35–100	Small church	Collie
100–175	Middle-sized	Garden
175–225	Awkward size	House
225–450	Large	Mansion
450–700	Huge	Ranch
700+	Minidenomination	Nation

In 1983 Schaller presented basic church size strategies to increase church membership in *Growing Plans*. This book is built around three major questions: How do small churches grow? How do middle-sized churches grow? How do large churches grow? Each of the chapters presents ideas for growth founded on size theory. Finally, writing in *The Very Large Church: New Rules for Leaders*, Schaller claims, ". . . next to the congregational culture, size is the most revealing and useful frame of reference for examining the differences among congregations in American Protestantism."[23]

Along with Schaller, an early church growth writer who influenced church size thinking was David A. Womack. In *The Pyramid Principle of Church Growth*, Womack introduced the concept that churches tend to cluster at certain sizes.

Building on earlier research by statistician George Edgerly, Womack wrote that churches tend to cluster at 35, 85, 125, 180, 240, 280, 400, 600, 800, and 1,200 average worshipers. The growth problem, according to Womack, is that churches do not expand their organization to fit the needs of the next size of church, and they plateau at predictable size levels. Thus he writes, "If a church wishes to serve more people, it must first expand its base of organization and ministry.[24]

While completing his study of the Church of the Nazarene for his doctoral program at Fuller Theological Seminary, Bill Sullivan became interested in the challenge of assisting churches to break the 200 barrier. A statistical analysis of Nazarene Churches in 1983 discovered that "nearly 90 percent have fewer than two hundred members. Indeed over half of the churches have fewer than seventy-five members."[25] After conducting further research to see what factors caused churches to remain below 200 in size, as well as how churches effectively broke the 200 barrier, in 1988 he published *Ten Steps to Breaking the 200 Barrier*. This book provided practical insights on how church leaders could manage the growth of a church beyond 200 in size. It was later revised and called *New Perspectives on Breaking the 200 Barrier*.

During the 1990s church consultant Carl George wrote two books based on the hypothesis that, as churches grow, they must change their organizational structure. *Prepare Your Church for the Future* focused on answering the question "How can a church be large enough to make a difference in the world while remaining small enough to care about people?" George shares: "Almost every growing church I've encountered faces insurmountable limits on its ability to expand its structure without serious disruption in quality." He further attests: "Churches find that each time they grow a little, their quality lessens, so they must scramble to implement a new organizational system geared to their current size."[26] The answer to this organizational dilemma, according to George, is to become a meta-church.

The name Meta-Church, then, is quite distinct from mega-church. This new label allows for greater numbers, but its deepest focus is on change: pastors' changing their minds about how ministry is to be done, and churches' changing their organizational form in order to be free from size constraints. A Meta-Church pastor understands how a church can be structured so that its most fundamental spiritual and emotional support centers never become obsolete, no matter how large it becomes.[27]

Meta-church theory calls for a new social architecture that is people-centered, ministry-centered, and care-centered. It builds on the analogy of yeasts (geometric growth of small groups over time), which allows for continual growth and personal care regardless of how large a church becomes. George says, "The Meta-Church can grow to any size without revising its social architecture for ministry or sacrificing quality of discipleship.[28]

Building on Schaller's analogy, George offers the following breakdown of churches by size.

Worship Attendance	Analogy
<35	Mouse-size church
35–75	Cat-size church
75–200	Lapdog-size church
200–1,000	Yard-dog-size church
1,000–3,000	Horse-size church
3,000–10,000	Elephant-size church
10,000+	Convention-of-mice meta-church[29]

At the time George wrote this book, fewer than fifteen churches had grown larger than 6,000 worshipers in the United States. He predicted, however, that "one day soon, North American churches of 25,000 to 50,000"[30] would appear in every metropolitan area, a prophecy that has come true in part. Leadership Network reported in January 2007 that there are 1,170 churches with worship attendances between 2,000 and 9,999, as well as 40 churches averaging more than 10,000 in worship attendance.[31]

In a follow-up book, *How to Break Growth Barriers*, Carl George deals specifically with the 200, 400, and 800 size barriers. He declares, "Churches have more in common by their size than by their denomination, tradition, location, age, or any other single, isolatable factor."[32] After demonstrating the predictable barriers, or sizes, around which churches cluster, he addresses several issues of organizational capacity necessary to break the 200 barrier: parking availability, space for classes and seating, and expansion/relocation. To pass the 400 barrier, George recommends changes in the roles of the board and staff. Essentially, operational functions must begin to be shifted to the staff, while policy-setting functions remain with the board. Growing beyond 800 requires changes in marketing, facilities usage, and organizational design. In part, leaders must establish reasonable spans of care, use niche marketing to reach new people, focus on life-stage ministry, and offer multiple worship services.[33]

Two other books appeared at the end of the 1990s by church growth authors that continued to enhance our understanding of church sizes. Elmer Towns, C. Peter Wagner, and Thom S. Rainer authored *The Everychurch Guide to Growth: How Any Plateaued Church Can Grow*. Wagner offered insights on breaking the 200 barrier, Rainer had ideas on breaking the middle-sized (400) barrier, and Towns wrote his thoughts on getting over the 1,000 barrier.[34] The second book, which I wrote in 1999, *One Size Doesn't Fit All: Bringing Out the Best in Any Size Church*, also addressed moving through the small, medium, and large forms of church. In this book I attempted to bring together all of the church growth thought up to that time related to small, medium, and large church size strategies.[35] Three recent books also reflect on the implication of size on church growth. *Overcoming Barriers to Growth* by Michael Fletcher submits that there are really only two barriers to the growth of a church: the 100/200 barrier and the 700/800 barrier.[36] Kevin E. Martin's book *The Myth of the 200 Barrier* takes a contrarian approach. He rejects the thesis of a 200 barrier, but espouses a dividing line (barrier?) at 150. Martin does admit that churches tend to cluster at predictable sizes.[37] While not strictly a study on church sizes, *Confessions of a Reformission Rev* is a testimony of how God worked in the ministry of Mars Hill Church in Seattle, Washington. The author, Mark Driscoll, writes, "Churches, like children, have a shoe size that they will grow into. As a church grows, it must accept its size."[38] The bulk of the book is a description of the challenges and changes that Mars Hill Church went through at predictable size levels: 0–45, 45–75, 75–150, 150–350, 350–1,000, 1,000–4,000, and 4,000–10,000.

A summary comparison of the breakdown of church sizes according to church growth writers shows how our understanding has developed over the years:

Schaller (1975)	Womack (1977)	Schaller (1980)	George (1991)	McIntosh (2009)
30–35	50	<35	35	35
70–85	90	35–100	50	85
115–135	120	100–175	100	125
175–200	200s	175–225	200	200
	300s	225–450	400	400
	600	450–700	800	800
	1,200	>700	1,000	1,200
			3,000	3,000
			6,000	6,000
			30,000	10,000

My listing above is not based on any scientifically gathered data, but a summary "best guess" based on the observations and studies I have read. Several researchers already mentioned above agree on the general barriers up to 800 in size. In his recent doctoral dissertation, David B. Vasquez confirms the existence of predictable clusters of churches at 1,200, 3,000, and 6,000 in size.[39] Leadership Network reports the following percentage of churches in the United States at various sizes as of 2007, which points to a possible barrier at 10,000.

Worship Attendance	Protestant Churches
1–99	177,000 (59 percent)
100–499	105,000 (35 percent)
500–999	12,000 (4 percent)
1,000–1,999	6,000 (2 percent)
2,000–9,999	1,170 (0.4 percent)
10,000+	40 (0.01 percent)

Based on research by John Vaughan, president of the Megachurch Research Center in Bolivar, Missouri, the following chart gives evidence that churches are continuing to grow above 2,000 in size and at a faster pace than ever.

Year	Total Megachurches (2,000 or more attendance)
1970	10
1980	50
1983	74
1985	100
1990	250
1998	400
2000	500
2003	700
2004	850
2005	1,200
2007	1,400

While it used to take a church from fifteen to fifty years to grow larger than 2,000 worshipers, it now appears to be happening in as little as five to ten years in several reported cases. Given current trends, we are most likely going to see even more large churches in the future. Thus it is crucial that we understand the dynamics of how larger organizations, including churches, grow.

How Churches Grow

The numerical growth of a local congregation does not take place in a smooth line or curve.[40] Rather it usually takes place through a series of plateaus or stair steps. Lyle Schaller explains: "There is a tendency to think of the growth (and the decline) of a congregation as resembling a smooth curve. Another way to look at it is to see the growth, or the decline, of a church as resembling a series of stair steps, with each step as a plateau."[41] Thus a church's growth may look similar to the figure below.

> It is crucial that we understand the dynamics of how larger organizations, including churches, grow.

FIGURE 32

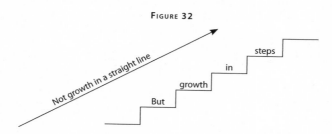

As noted earlier in this chapter, studies completed over the last quarter century found that churches tend to cluster at predictable size levels as they grow. Lyle Schaller was the first to point this out when he wrote, "There is a tendency for congregations to cluster around several points that can be described as steps or plateaus."[42] My review of the research demonstrates that normally churches in the United States cluster at ten plateau levels.

FIGURE 33

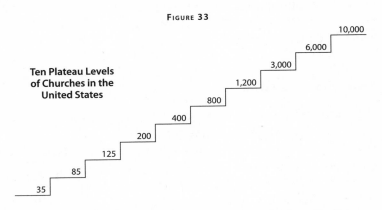

Ten Plateau Levels
of Churches in the
United States

10,000
6,000
3,000
1,200
800
400
200
125
85
35

Each congregation, of course, is a unique body of believers. One congregation will travel up and down the stair steps in a way that is distinct from that of another. Yet at each step enough common patterns are observable to allow forecasts of what must be done to allow for continued growth.

Basically, a church's structure allows it to grow to a certain level, after which the church plateaus unless appropriate changes are made. At each step or plateau, a transition in the nature of the organization must occur if the church is to continue to grow to the following step or plateau.

Of Barriers and Plateaus

As described above there is a dynamic relationship between church size and structure.[43] Leading and managing different sized churches requires changing sets of skills and knowledge. Each plateau acts like a floor and a ceiling in a building. The floor offers support, while the ceiling offers resistance.

A church often plateaus as it bounces between the ceiling and the floor. This produces the long-term plateauing

130

FIGURE 34

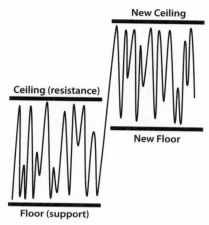

effect that is often observed in churches. If a church is able to grow beyond the plateau or ceiling, it then settles onto a new plateau with a new ceiling and floor. The points at which churches tend to cluster are not hard numerical numbers, nor are they solid like floors and ceilings, but rather are "ranges" of numbers around which churches tend to cluster. For example, the 200 plateau is not a hard number, but is more of a range, say between 150 and 250. Thus a church that plateaus at 150 is still struggling with the 200 barrier, as is the church that plateaus at 250.[44]

Size barriers are not hard objects to be broken but a hill to be climbed. Consider what happens when a driver approaches a hill in a car. As the car comes closer to the hill the driver gradually pushes on the gas pedal thereby giving the car additional energy to make it up the hill. Once the car makes it over the hill and onto level ground, the driver can reduce the pressure on the gas pedal, as it takes less energy to travel on level ground than up a hill. When a church attempts to take it to the next size level, more energy is required to make the climb before it settles onto the next plateau. The new burst of energy is the adjustment in the or-

Each climb is at once a result of the previous climb and a preparation for the next.

ganizational structure. David Womack says, "Each increase in congregational size demands a corresponding shift in the operational base. Many churches have failed to grow because they have not understood this simple rule: Organizational expansion always precedes numerical increase."[45] Each climb is at once a result of the previous climb and a preparation for the next.

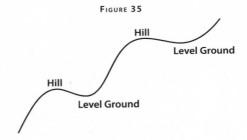

FIGURE 35

Though I have identified ten plateau levels for churches, I find it most helpful to place them in five descriptive categories: relational church, managerial church, organizational church, centralized church, and decentralized church. These five church categories are described in chapters 11 through 15. Each chapter paints a picture of what organizational changes are necessary at each level if a church desires to take it to the next level.

What's Happening?

1. Based on the size categories found in figure 33, "Ten Plateau Levels of Churches in the United States" on page 130, where does your church currently fit?

132

2. Has your church ever been larger or smaller than it is currently? If so, describe ways that it was different at each size level?

3. Looking at your church's past growth history, does it tend to plateau at a predictable size? If so, why do you think it stops growing at that size?

11

The Relational Church

15 to 200 Worshipers

Half of the congregations in North America need to expand
their weekend worship services.

Lyle E. Schaller

As Phil, Mike, and Wes continued their conversation, Phil
declared, "I don't ever remember being taught any of this
in school."

"Me either," Wes agreed. "After graduating, my thought
was always, *slow and steady*; that is, I thought my church's
growth would be in a smooth straight line. I didn't realize
we'd plateau at a certain level and get stuck there."

"Whether we call them barriers or plateaus," Mike said,
"my experience causes me to believe that churches do stop
growing at certain sizes."

"I agree. It seems that most research points out that there
are clear plateaus at which churches gather," Wes said. "Al-

most every book I've read on this subject says that up to 80 or 85 percent of churches never grow larger than 200 people."

"What does it take to grow beyond 200 at worship?" Phil asked. "One year we had an Easter Sunday attendance of over 300, and I thought we'd broken through the so-called 200 barrier. We had to bring in lots of extra chairs. People were even sitting in the aisles. Unfortunately we couldn't sustain that large an attendance and quickly fell back to our regular worship attendance of about 115 within a few weeks."

"I don't know the answer," Mike answered. "As I mentioned earlier, my church opened with more than 200 people on the first Sunday. The following week we dropped down to about 100 in attendance and worked up from there. Looking back at it now, we did move to a new location that had more parking and seating, and at the same time we added a second full-time staff member and a couple of secretaries, but other than that the growth beyond 200 in size seemed to happened on its own."

Wes broke in. "But it didn't happen on its own. You moved to a new location, added parking, seating, and additional staff personnel."

"That's right. We did," Mike agreed.

"What would have happened if you had not moved or had not added more staff or had not increased your parking and seating?" Wes asked.

"We wouldn't have grown past 200," Mike said. "We just didn't have the capacity to hold more people or to relate to them."

"Maybe that's our problem!" Phil seemed excited. "My church has never had more than one pastor. Our auditorium seats only 125 comfortably, and I've never had a full-time secretary."

Because of their size, most churches are in the *relational church* category; church researchers generally locate 80 percent of all churches in this size category,[1] which includes all churches that average 200 or fewer persons at their primary worship services. The descriptive term *relational* gives the key to this group of churches. Even though churches averaging 35 or 85 or 200 persons at worship on a given Sunday morning are different, the factor that ties them together is their focus on relationships.

Characteristics

Generally, churches under 200 in size have a bivocational or solo pastor. In the past it was assumed that a church of about 50 people could support a full-time pastor and provide for a basic ministry program. Normally this meant 12 people or families donated their full tithe to the church. In today's economic environment this old assumption does not work out quite as well as it once did. Churches are discovering that they need at least two to three times that number of worshipers and people giving a tithe to provide a pastor a full-time salary and full benefits, as well as having enough money left over to provide a subsistence level of programming. Thus churches with fewer than 150 worshipers often find they must employ the services of a bivocational pastor or perhaps pay a pastor a lower than average wage.[2]

> Churches with fewer than 150 worshipers often find they must employ the services of a bivocational pastor or perhaps pay a pastor a lower than average wage.

Members of relational churches see the pastor's primary calling as that of a caregiver. The core values of smaller churches cause them to look for a highly relational pastor who serves church members by listening to their concerns, ministering to their personal needs, and following their lead. Thus pastors are not thought of as leaders in a relational church but simply as caregivers. The *de facto* leaders are the persons, families, or small cohorts of people who have supported the church over many years and have wielded decision-making authority. Tight-knit relationships tie these key persons together, and they often comprise the majority of board members who view the pastor as their hired hand rather than their leader.

The church's management structure is somewhat haphazard. Management decisions are often made outside of formal meetings, but meetings are used when the leaders find them helpful in maintaining control. Long-range planning is not considered a necessity; thus plans are made at the last minute and the quality of the ministry often reflects this last-minute planning.

Leaders are selected based on their ties or support of the controlling family or cohort. Rarely are newcomers chosen to serve in any significant manner until it is determined that they are safe, meaning that long-term church leaders trust them. Since the pool from which leaders are selected is quite small, leaders normally have limited abilities—they are chosen on the basis of availability rather than giftedness or skill sets.

Key Points of Transition

Some people view the steps at which churches plateau as definite points of transition; however, it is more helpful to see each step as more of a range of size than a specific size. For example, the most widely known plateau point is the 200 barrier, but we rarely find a church plateaued at exactly 200 in size. As I pointed out in the last chapter, this level includes a wide range of churches, from those averaging 150 to those averaging 250. For now it is important to understand that each key point of transition is more of a range than a precise point. We can identify three of these levels in the relational church, and those desiring to grow beyond the three levels must do the following.

Growing from 35 to 85

The main key that allows a church to move from the first level to the second (see figure 33, "Ten Plateau Levels of Churches in the United States" on page 130) is adding a full-time pastor. Seldom will a church grow beyond 35 people with a bivocational pastor. The only time a pastor serving a church in such a limited way results in a growing church is during the initial phases of a church plant. Even then, if the founding pastor continues too long in a bivocational capacity, the new church has a greater than even chance of experiencing limited growth. A church of this size must find a way to obtain the services of a full-time pastor if it expects to go to the next level.

When a church has only 35 people in attendance, a pastor must be able to model the ministry by serving as an example to the congregation. The pastor will need to cast vision for the future by speaking publicly *and* person to person. In most cases it will be the pastor's personal skills that are most effective in leading the church to the next level.

People expect churches to provide a basic level of programming. At the very minimum, people expect a church to provide a worship service and a basic children's program. While a house church, normally comprised of fewer than 35 people, can get along with almost no children's ministry, once a church grows larger than 35, expectations begin to increase. To move from 35 to 85 people in attendance, a church must develop a nursery and preschool, kindergarten, and early elementary classes.

There is a need to draw a critical mass of worshipers to the service. In most churches this means reaching a minimum attendance of 50 people. The larger a church gets, the more people expect the worship service to feel dynamic. No one expects a church of between 35 and 85 to be as dynamic as a larger one, but it usually takes at least 50 people before, for example, the singing in the worship service reaches a moderate level of excitement. Since a church needs musicians,

138

worship leaders, and child care workers, the attendance must get to about 65 total participants to have a critical mass of 50 people in the audience.

Finding a facility that will allow the church to expand is still another key element in moving to the next level of ministry. Often the lack of adequate seating, parking, and classroom meeting space holds many smaller churches on a plateau for a long period of time. For a church to reach an average of 85 worshipers, it must have a facility that seats between 100 and 125. In addition there must be a minimum of 40 to 50 parking spaces available during the worship time. Without this minimum level of available seating and parking, it will be nearly impossible for a church to average 85 people in worship attendance.

To move to the next level, the church will have to grow beyond one large family. In many smaller churches it is not unusual to find that nearly all the members of the church are related to one another. A church made up of one matriarch and patriarch, their four children, and their spouses and children can easily add up to 20 to 25 persons. Add on their close friends and you have the basic 35-member church. It stands to reason then that if such a church is to grow to the next level of 85 people, it must add people outside the family cohort group. This may be the biggest challenge in the smallest churches. Small family churches of this sort find it difficult to open their arms to people who are not family members. The old saying "We're just a big happy family" means more than fellowship in these smallest of churches.

Growing from 85 to 125

To reach the third level of 125, more ministry programs must be added. As a church approaches this size, people will begin to increase their expectations, particularly at the adult level. When the church was smaller, most likely the adults found that the worship service met their needs. The small family feel allowed adults to know everyone in an intimate way. They could pray for one another and serve each other without much effort. Most people, studies confirm, can know only about sixty persons on a first-name basis. Thus when a church grows beyond that number of participants, people begin to feel left out. Normally, to reach the next level of 125, a church must add three new adult programs that relate to men and women.

Expectations for children's programming increase as well. Children's classes up to sixth grade are needed at this new size level. Some may wish for a youth ministry but the critical mass of youth is often too small to provide a youth program at this size. Additional ministry offerings outside of Sunday morning may also be needed, but some churches find they can make use of a children's program at another church for activities during the week.

When a church grows beyond 85 people, it is a prime time to begin a small-group ministry. The church is now large enough that a single fellowship meeting of the entire church is not easy to accomplish, but the desire of people for connection will provide an opportunity to bring people together in homes. A church should plan to offer a minimum of seven small groups for every 100 adults in worship attendance.

By this point the pastor will certainly be full-time. While he continues to model ministry, it is critical that the pastor begin delegating ministry to others, as well. The church is still small enough that most worshipers will want contact with the pastor, and this can be difficult unless help is given by hiring a good secretary for him. This move can assist in propelling the church to the next size level.

Once again the need for adequate facilities becomes crucial. For a church to have an average attendance of 125 in one worship service means they need a minimum seating capacity of 150. Add to this the need for 70 parking spaces, and it is easy to see how the lack of an adequate facility can cause a church to plateau.

Growing from 125 to beyond 200

Breaking the proverbial 200 barrier has proven to be the biggest growth challenge that churches face. Over the last quarter century more research has focused on how to grow beyond this level than on any of the other nine levels combined. There are at least nine key factors that must be implemented before a church is able to break this most difficult barrier, and three of them are related to the pastor.

ADD STAFF

To grow beyond 125, a church must add a second full-time pastor and two full-time support staff. Recent studies confirm that churches grow at a rate equal to around 150 people for every full-time pastor.[3] Given this reality, it is clear that, for a church to grow beyond 200 worshipers, it must have two pastors. The newest finding, however, is the need to have an equal number of support staff in place. Research completed by David Vasquez in 2006 found that growing churches have one support staff for each full-time pastoral staff.

> **Growing churches have one support staff for each full-time pastoral staff.**

Figuring out the number of staff that are needed is the easy part, of course. It is finding the money to pay them that is the hard part. It is a catch-22 situation. To break the 200 barrier a church needs extra staff members, but at the church's current size, it does not have the money to hire them. It is at this point that a church must become creative. My research has found that churches address this need through several means. For instance, churches use volunteer staff, pay some at below-market wages, hire several part-time staff members, recruit staff members who can pay their own way, ask for financial gifts to cover extra staff, expect staff members to raise support outside the church, and use a number of other creative options.

Expect an Administrative Shepherd

For the church to continue to grow, the lead pastor must shift from operating primarily as a caregiving shepherd to being more of an administrative shepherd. For most pastors this has proven to be a difficult change in leadership style. The fact that 80 percent of churches are still smaller than 200 indicates that most pastors are not able to make this shift. Or perhaps it shows that the congregation will not allow the pastor to make such a change in leadership style. However, as a church grows larger than 200 people, it requires that the senior pastor begin overseeing the larger church program, which will include more administrative work.

Delegate Ministry

If the church is to grow, the pastor must begin delegating ministry to other leaders in the church—lay leaders as well as paid staff members. When a church grows beyond 200, it becomes evident that a pastor cannot do it all. History shows that when a pastor tries to do it all and does not learn to delegate to others, the church will stop growing. Delegation skills are not taught to pastors in most Christian colleges, universities, and seminaries but must be learned in the field by pastors. Those who learn to delegate and do so find their churches growing beyond 200.

Mobilize Laypeople

Another important change is to mobilize lay members of the congregation. For a pastor to delegate ministry to others, the church must teach members to discover and use their spiritual gifts, as well as their natural talents. Growing beyond 200 requires that more ministry programs are started, and it will take the wise recruitment, training, and deploying of laity for this to happen.

CONTINUALLY EXPAND PROGRAMMING

Continual expansion of the ministry program is necessary if the church is to grow. As a church nears 200 in size and passes that mark, people begin to expect the church to have a youth program for junior high or middle school students and high school students. The youth pastor, however, should not be the second pastor added to the staff. At this point in the growth of the church, it is best if the youth ministry is in the hands of volunteers.

ADD A SECOND WORSHIP SERVICE

In most churches it will also take the addition of a second worship service for a church to pass the 200 barrier. While this depends to some degree on the size of the worship auditorium, studies of churches that have grown larger than 200 point to the fact that most added a second worship service as part of their growth mix.[4] New worship services reach new people for Christ by offering a new style of worship, a new time for worship, and sometimes a new day for worship, all of which help a church grow.

ADD CLASSES

Churches that wish to grow must add new groups and classes. People need places to gather so they can serve, care, and support each other. The larger a church becomes, the more difficult it is to meet adult needs through the worship service alone. It takes more groups to reach more people. In general, a church of 200 should have a minimum of 6 adult classes or other mid-sized groups, along with 14 smaller groups. The smaller groups should be a variety of some Bible studies, some support groups, and some activity groups, based on the context of the church and its people.

MAINTAIN A SIMPLE DECISION-MAKING STRUCTURE

While adding staff, lay leaders, a worship service, groups, and classes, it is important for a church to maintain a level of simplicity in the decision-making structure. The organization's structure must become more formal but it should not be allowed to become bureaucratic in a way that stifles creativity and the ease of making decisions.

EXPAND FACILITIES

Expanding facilities is a continuing need as a church grows to the next size level. If the church has only one worship service, it will need a minimum of 110 parking spaces and a minimum seating capacity of 250. Add to this additional rooms for child care, youth, and adult classes, and it is easy to see why expanding the facilities is a continuing issue for growing churches.

Using these key factors of growth as guidelines, local congregations will be able to transition beyond the size levels found in most relational churches. However, since churches are unique bodies, these insights may not be the answer for all churches; they should be helpful to about 90 percent of churches below the 200 size level.

What's Happening?

1. What characteristics of your church indicate that it fits into the relational church category?
2. To which challenges, presented in this chapter, do you relate to the most? Why?
3. List three of the ideas from this chapter that you can begin to work on this year.

12

The Managerial Church

200 to 400 Worshipers

The important thing is this: to be able to give up in any given moment all that we are for what we can become.

DeSeaux

"As I mentioned," Mike was saying, "my church grew past 200 worshipers quickly, but we plateaued with about 350 people for three years."

"What happened? Why did your church stop growing at that point?" Phil asked.

"It's hard to be specific, but my biggest challenge," Mike admitted, "was changing my style of leadership. I'm a visionary type of leader and I don't really care to do much administration, but church administration started taking up a lot of my time. Overnight we added several committees and I was an ex officio member of them all. After a while all I was doing was attending meetings."

Looking frustrated, Wes said, "I know what that feels like. At one of the churches I served there were way too many committees. I had some committee meeting nearly every day. Unfortunately most of the important decisions regarding the church's ministry were made in the committees, so I had to be there."

"I know," Mike agreed reluctantly. "Another challenge we faced was an uncertain feeling about what type of church we were."

"I don't understand." Phil seemed confused.

"Well, let me put it this way, some people wanted us to act like a small church, and others wanted us to act like a large church. Our frustration came about because we were too big to provide the close relational feel common to smaller churches, but at the same time we were not large enough to provide the numerous programs that larger churches offer. We knew we weren't a small church or a large one but we didn't know what we were."

"I'd say you were a middle-sized church." Phil grinned.

"True, but what's a middle-sized church?" Mike asked. "Everyone knows what a small church is like and what a large church is like, but it's difficult to determine what a middle-sized church is like."

The conversation of the three pastor friends focuses on what may be the most difficult aspect of serving a middle-sized church—defining its identity. A small church is known for its relational structure. People have close, face-to-face friendships, which result in the feeling of being a happy family. On the other hand, larger churches are known for the large number and variety of programs, which allow for nearly anyone to find a place that ministers to their needs or affinities. A middle-sized church is neither small nor large and is therefore hard to define.

Characteristics

Middle-sized churches are characterized by their organizational structure. As a church grows larger than 200 worshipers, the essential nature of the church changes from focusing on relationships to organizing its growing array of new ministries, people, staff, and facility. Of course developing relationships continues to be a major aspect of the church's overall ministry, but the growth in size brings with it the need to administer the church in a better way.

Pastors who flourish in a church of between 200 to 400 in size are often gifted administrators or they are able to function well in an administrative capacity for a brief period of time. It is possible for pastors who are strong caregivers to lead middle-sized churches, but they will need to share leadership with an administrative assistant or an assistant pastor who will handle the bulk of administrative details.

The small staff and volunteer leaders in the middle-sized church are good at doing ministry but some of them find it difficult to build teams and they end up doing most of the work themselves. If the pastor and other leaders do not learn to delegate, this phase of the church's life will wear them out.

Organizational structure must be fluid as the church wrestles with putting in place a new way of doing things.

Organizational structure must be fluid as the church wrestles with putting in place a new way of doing things. Leaders find that the grapevine doesn't work as well in getting information disseminated among the members, and decisions have to be made through formal channels. New policies are developed for auditing financial books, selecting leaders, and starting new ministries.

At this size, the decision-making authority begins moving away from the family cohort model that is observed in smaller churches. Historically, as churches reached this phase, a struc-

147

ture of committee or commissions took the place of the ruling family model for decision making. Today most churches try to avoid the committee structure if at all possible, preferring to delegate decision making to individuals.

Transition Pressures

Like churches found at every level of growth, some middle-sized churches hover for years at their plateau of between 200 and 400 worshipers. Those that stay at this level for a long time experience continual pressures due to pulls in two opposite directions.

FIGURE 36

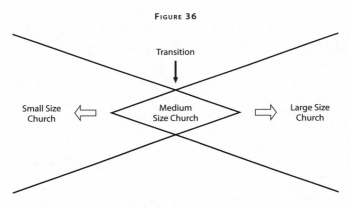

Staying on a plateau at this level for a long time is difficult. People who prefer a smaller church environment issue calls for a return to a simpler church where everyone can know each other. This may take the form of a request to eliminate multiple worship services in favor of returning to one service. Or it may come as a stated hope for more personal visits from the pastor or even eliminating a staff member in the guise of cutting costs. Whatever form it takes, there will be regular pressure to return the church to one that has the relational characteristics of churches with fewer than 200 worshipers.

148

Other pressures come from people who prefer a larger church. They may request an increased variety and number of ministry options, perhaps arising from real needs people are facing in their personal lives. For example, a family with a special needs child may ask for programming to meet their particular need. Single adults may request a program designed specifically for their concerns. Younger adults may expect the church to offer a more contemporary worship service on a Saturday evening. The possibilities are endless, but the pressures mount as some worshipers desire the church to move on to become a larger church.

Due to such pressures, most middle-sized churches move in one of the two directions. Over time they will either continue to grow, becoming a larger church, or succumb eventually to the pull to return to the small church model. Often decisions made at this size level set the direction of a church for many years.

Key Points of Transition

Churches that grow beyond 400 worshipers make the following moves.

Add Staff

When churches at this level want to grow, they add a third full-time pastor plus one additional support staff member. This brings the paid staff to three pastors and three support people. Since each pastor can effectively serve 150 people, 3 pastoral staff members are needed to grow beyond 400 (3 x 150 = 450). A church cannot wait until it has an attendance of 450 before hiring the third person. It is the addition of the third pastor that allows the church to grow beyond 400 worshipers. In some situations it may even demand the addition of a fourth staff person, particularly if there are heavy demands made of the staff, which may occur if the church does not hire support staff equal to the number of pastors. In this case the pastor is able to minister effectively to only 125 people, rather than 150 people, meaning three pastors can serve only about 375 people. In such situations the church will either have to hire additional support staff or a fourth pastor to grow larger than 400.

Senior Pastor Becomes Leader

For a church to grow beyond 400, the senior pastor must begin thinking and functioning as a leader more than an administrator. While serving a middle-sized church, the function of the ministry required him to think and act like an administrator, as the church grows larger, the pastor must make another transition to function as a leader. Among other things, this means the pastor becomes responsible for long-range planning, directing a multiple staff, casting a vision for the future of the church, preaching consistently fine sermons, and designing systems to reach, win, and keep new people.

> **For a church to grow beyond 400, the senior pastor must begin thinking and functioning as a leader more than an administrator.**

Laypersons Take Responsibility

The church must also start the process of shifting responsibility for pastoral care from the pastors to laypersons. As the total number of worshipers increases, it becomes more and more difficult for pastors to maintain a high level of quality care for the entire congregation. The growing administrative, leadership, and training roles of the pastors make it increasingly difficult to maintain contact with every member, and the larger numbers of people attending worship services make it more difficult to keep track of the members. This process takes time to develop but it must begin to be implemented as the church passes the 400 mark.

Roles of Staff Change

Another shift that begins at this level is changing the roles and responsibilities of the staff. As the senior pastor transitions into more of a leadership role, other pastors and support staff shift into more specialized roles covering administration, outreach, newcomer connection, children, youth, and adult ministry. If the early pastoral staff were considered generalists, they now become specialists.

Add Worship Service

To move beyond 400 worshipers, most churches will need to add a third worship service. The variable is the size of the worship center, but a church with two worship services must have a minimum of 325 usable seats in its auditorium to maintain an attendance above 400 at two services. If a church has seating for only 200 people, it will have to add a third worship service to have any chance of breaking the 400 barrier. In addition, a church seating 200 people and with three worship services requires a minimum of 150 parking spaces to break 400 in attendance.

Build on Success

The church identifies and builds on its stars. A careful look at a church will reveal that a limited number of people, programs, and priorities are advancing it forward. Commonly called the 80/20 rule, it may be stated thus: 20 percent of your effort gives you 80 percent of your results. This principle means that 20 percent of your members will win 80 percent of your converts. Twenty percent of your people will donate 80 percent of your income. Twenty percent of your ministries will attract 80 percent of your new people.

One of the keys to taking your church to the next level is to identify the 20 percent of people and ministries that are responsible for your church's growth and build on them. For example, if you discover that a particular ministry is bringing in a majority of your newcomers, then you will want to invest more in that ministry. Identifying your stars and investing in making them even more fruitful will help propel your church to the next level.

What's Happening?

1. Is your church at the level of a managerial church? How do you know?
2. Which of the key transition points do you need to begin working on this year?
3. Can you identify your ministry stars? Which programs, ministries, and/or people are responsible for bringing most of the new growth to your church? How can you invest in these stars to empower more growth in the future?

13

The Organizational Church

400 to 800 Worshipers

I will go anywhere, as long as it's forward.

David Livingston

"Well," Phil forged ahead while Mike and Wes seemed to be in deep thought. "You obviously grew past the 400 plateau. What happened after that?"

Mike didn't answer right away, struggling to get his thoughts together. "Actually, I found that my gifts fit a larger church better than the middle-size church," Mike said. "The best picture I can draw is to say that I was like a player coach. I still had to be in the game doing ministry but I found myself coaching other members of the staff and board to take over areas of ministry."

"What was your biggest hurdle, Mike?" asked Wes.

"Without a doubt," Mike answered quickly, "it was the bureaucratic nature of our church. The committee structure we established when the church was smaller worked well for a while, but the larger we grew, the more that structure held us back. It just took too long to make decisions."

"In that church I pastored that had all the committees, four different committees had to sign off on any new program," Wes said and the others smiled. "We finally changed our church's structure to have only one board that decided everything."

"Our board structure was part of the bureaucratic mess too," Mike added. "Not only did most decisions have to go through our committees, but they also had to receive the blessing of our board. I found myself working overtime trying to guide new programs through our system. The board seemed to veto about everything that came their way. It was exceedingly difficult."

"What about your staff?" Phil asked with a look of dismay. "I'd think your staff would make many of the decisions and work with the various committees so you wouldn't need to."

"Even though I had a multiple staff, everyone came to me for decisions. My staff members were very competent practitioners but they couldn't make decisions on their own," Mike said.

"So what did you do?"

"We gradually realigned the staff and slowly began making changes to our organizational structure. The truth is we are still in the process of deciding what it will take to get us to the next level of ministry."

One of the transitions that takes place as a church plateaus between 400 and 800 in size is the way the senior pastor is viewed by the congregation. At the relational church level the pastor is seen as the one responsible for giving care to others. Then, as the church reaches the managerial church size, people recognize the need for better administration, and often the pastor moves into that role. Once a church breaks the 400 barrier, the pastor takes the role of a player coach. At this level people understand that the pastor is a leader, but lingering expectations require the pastor to stay personally involved in a number of ways. Often people who have attended the church for years feel this way. His age and experience give him a special standing among other staff members, which allows him to stand alongside the staff and give them advice. However, there will still be times when he must be directly involved in ministry.

Characteristics

Staff organization and relationships develop slowly as a church grows. In the early years a church appoints a second and third pastor in an effort to give the senior pastor help in caring for the congregation. As additional staff members are added through the years, each one is expected to report directly to the senior pastor. Gradually the pastor becomes the center of every staff member's attention, as they go to him for advice, coaching, and decision making. The senior pastor becomes the "hub of the wheel" (as in the figure below). This arrangement of staff works well when a church and its staff are small, with perhaps seven staff members, but as the staff grows, it becomes difficult for the pastor to relate directly to each staff member.

FIGURE 37

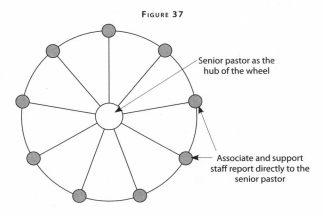

Senior pastor as the hub of the wheel

Associate and support staff report directly to the senior pastor

155

In the early years of a church's growth, particularly when the church has fewer than 400 in worship attendance, staff members are hired to "do" ministry. The first staff members are expected to be competent practitioners. For example, a children's pastor works directly with the children, a visitation pastor is expected to visit people, and a youth pastor is appointed to spend personal time with the youth. As a church grows beyond 400 in worship attendance, expectations of staff members begin to change. No longer is their main concern the doing of ministry; now it becomes critical that they build teams of people to help them do ministry. The problem is that doing ministry and building teams require different sets of skills. Some staff members may make the transition well, but others may struggle.

Management structure in an organizational church is usually bureaucratic. A managerial church (200–400) organizes by placing people onto committees. Typically, each major area of ministry—youth, worship, missions, education, care, outreach, and administration—has a group of people assigned to oversee it. While this management approach involves a large number of people, over time the committees become bureaucratic and effectively impede ministry development, as too many cooks in the kitchen spoil the food. Unless the church reorganizes to reflect the dynamic of a larger church, the ministry may grind to a halt.

> **Unless the church reorganizes to reflect the dynamic of a larger church, the ministry may grind to a halt.**

When smaller churches design their initial board structures, members are recruited to make decisions on behalf of the church. This works well because the church is small enough that board members can meet once or twice a month for a limited amount of time, understand the needs of the ministry, and make appropriate decisions. However, as the church grows larger, it becomes increasingly difficult for a board to grasp the significance of everything that takes place in the church. Meetings start taking more time and the board meets more often as it attempts to gain a good enough understanding of the issues to make wise decisions. As might be expected, decisions take longer to make, and the church ministry slows down. In some churches the board is so slow in making decisions that they gain a reputation for not being able to make up their minds.

Key Points of Transition

For a church to grow beyond the 800 level, at least five key points of transition must be addressed.

Pastor's Role

The church must begin to define the pastor's role as that of leader rather than manager or caregiver. The congregation and lay leaders must come to the realization and acceptance of the fact that the pastor simply cannot do it all. Members of the congregation who prefer a smaller or middle-sized church need to release the small and medium-sized church mentalities that expect the pastor to be personally involved in everyone's lives or to administer every detail of the church's organizational structure.

> **The church must begin to define the pastor's role as that of leader rather than manager or caregiver.**

Team of Specialists

The staff team must change from being a group of practitioners, who are good at doing the ministry, to a team of specialists, who are excellent at designing ministries, which they lead. No longer are staff needed who are able only to do the ministry themselves. Staff must be able to build a larger program or ministry around their particular specialty.

Leadership Development

The church must begin to focus on leadership development. In large part the church will not grow unless additional leaders are developed to help support the enlarging program. If the church continues to grow, but leaders are not developed, eventually leaders will burn out. As leaders burn out, programs will collapse and the church will decline.

New Ministry Development

For a church to grow beyond 800, it must develop new ministries, programs, groups, and classes. One way of doing this is for the church to identify new niches to reach people for Christ. As newcomers start attending the church, they bring with them new needs, interests, and desires. A church will grow as it identifies the new needs and builds ministries to meet them.

Caregiving by Laypersons

For a church to grow larger than 800, it must shift caregiving from the pastoral staff to laypersons. This is by far the most important transition point to be made. As the church grows, staff members will not be able to keep up with the personal needs that people bring to the church. There will be too many people needing counseling and too many people in the hospital for the pastoral staff to take care of them all. Essentially, caregiving must become the focus of the laypeople. This means empowering small-group leaders, teachers, and volunteers to be "pastors" of small flocks of people in the church. Thus a worship team leader is *more* than a worship leader. He or she is the pastor of the worship team. A Bible study leader is *more* than a Bible teacher, becoming the pastor of the people in the study.

Growing beyond 800 takes concerted effort for the church to realign staff roles and responsibilities, as well as redesign the organizational structure to allow for faster decision making and responsive pastoral care for the entire congregation.

What's Happening?

1. What characteristics of the organizational church can you identify in your church? Name them specifically.
2. What key points of transition do you see as important for the growth of your church?
3. Which transition points will you begin to work on this month?

14

The Centralized Church

800 to 1,500 Worshipers

I never want to feel I've learned the best way how. There's always one hill higher with a better view.

Art Fettig

"Getting back to my original problem," Mike was saying to Phil and Wes, "my church is stuck between 1,000 and 1,200 worshipers. We worked our way through each of the previous levels, but neither I nor my board know what to do now."

"I used to serve on the staff of a larger church as executive pastor," Wes recalled. "As I remember, the pastor pretty much set the agenda for the church and the board supported him."

"Did the pastor make all of the decisions?" Mike inquired.

"No, the staff made the day-to-day decisions and they had to work within the policies that were set by the church board,"

Wes answered, "but the board expected the senior pastor and the staff to make most of the functional decisions."

"How was the staff organized?" Mike asked.

"Even though I was the executive pastor," Wes replied, "we had an executive team. Each member built their own ministry team, with each one organized much like divisions in a company."

"Sounds like your church was very centralized," Phil interjected.

"It was centralized around the pastoral staff team more than anything else. In fact one of our problems was that we tended to get so involved in our ministry divisions that we didn't always cooperate well together."

"What other issues did you struggle with?" Mike asked.

"The complexity of the church was a major issue. The larger the church became, the more complex and difficult it was to coordinate. We had to design mundane systems for about everything. We couldn't afford to leave anything to chance. I'll say this, the church expected our senior pastor to set a clear direction for the church. It's funny, but a lot of the people never came in contact with the senior pastor except on Sunday mornings. Everything he did on Sunday morning took on an extremely crucial aspect. If he had a bad sermon, we'd see a decline in attendance the next week."

"Ouch!" Phil said. "That's a lot of pressure. At least in my church everyone sees me and knows I love them."

"That's true," Wes agreed. "In the centralized church, though, the only thing most people know about the senior pastor is how good he is at preaching."

Characteristics

As a church grows larger, its complexity increases. This results in several characteristics that differ from those of smaller churches.

The Pastor as Visionary

> **In the centralized church the pastor takes on the role of a visionary.**

In the centralized church the pastor takes on the role of a visionary. People in the largest churches expect the pastor to cast a vision for the future of the church. If the senior pastor doesn't point the way to the future, people will wonder what's wrong. Thus the pastor must be a strategic thinker or at least build a team around him that can assist in the development of strategy.

When a church is small, the people know the pastor so intimately that they forgive days when the sermon may not be the best. However, when a church grows beyond 1,200, the people don't have a close personal relationship with the senior pastor. This means the only thing people know about the pastor is how well he preaches and leads from the platform on the weekend. The sermon takes on a very crucial aspect, for if the sermon doesn't connect with people, they may not remain at the church, since that is about all they really know about him.

Multiple-Level Staff

The staff of this size church changes from being a multiple staff to a multiple-level staff. Basically, a church that has a multiple staff has a senior pastor and some staff members. In the largest churches, however, there is a multiple-level staff. For example, a church may have a young adult pastor who oversees the college, high school, and middle school ministries. He may have his own staff of a college pastor, a high school pastor, and a middle school pastor under him. Thus the young adult pastor is on a pastoral team as well as having his own team—this is a multiple-level staff.

Decision-Making Authority of Staff

As a church grows larger, it becomes increasingly difficult for the board to make decisions about church ministry, so decision-making authority is vested in the staff. Of course the board will always have a major say in how the overall church runs, but the day-to-day decisions are transferred to the staff. Lead staff members will have great authority in deciding how to conduct the ministry under their care and will set the direction for its future, apart from oversight by a committee or board. Staff members report directly to the pastor who is over their area, with everyone essentially under the oversight of the senior pastor and the executive team.

Pastor Directed and Board Protected

Considering the above characteristics, we can describe the centralized church as pastor directed and board protected. These large churches begin to notice that they need a single voice before the congregation. Since the senior pastor has the primary platform before the entire congregation, this role naturally falls to him. Churches that grow to this size are ones in which the board of directors trusts the senior pastor to set direction, allows him to do so, and protects him from those in the church who may be overly critical of the direction he sets.

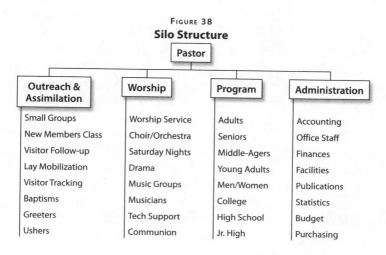

FIGURE 38
Silo Structure

Pastor			
Outreach & Assimilation	**Worship**	**Program**	**Administration**
Small Groups	Worship Service	Adults	Accounting
New Members Class	Choir/Orchestra	Seniors	Office Staff
Visitor Follow-up	Saturday Nights	Middle-Agers	Finances
Lay Mobilization	Drama	Young Adults	Facilities
Visitor Tracking	Music Groups	Men/Women	Publications
Baptisms	Musicians	College	Statistics
Greeters	Tech Support	High School	Budget
Ushers	Communion	Jr. High	Purchasing

Management Divisions

The management structure of the centralized church is focused in divisions, or what some call silos (see figure 38 on page 163). Each area of ministry develops around a pastor who specializes in that particular field of ministry. Each associate pastor builds a ministry that specializes in his or her chosen field of interest. A multiple-level staff is developed within each division and they work mostly within their division.

Key Points of Transition

Taking a church beyond the 1,500 level requires the following transition points.

Adjust Roles of Board and Staff

One of the key changes a church must make as it grows beyond 1,500 is adjusting the roles of the board and staff. Board functions must be separated from staff functions. Essentially, the board has to let go of making the everyday, functional decisions regarding church ministry, programs, staff, budget, and a host of other issues related to the work of the church. This is an especially difficult change to bring about due to the fact that most likely the board has been involved in making such decisions in the past. However, if a board seeks to maintain control over day-to-day decisions, as the church grows more complex, it will keep the church from growing beyond 1,500 in size.

The church board must become a policy-setting board and allow the staff to begin making functional ministry decisions within the policies the board sets. Among other things, this means the board must focus on deciding larger issues related to the overall budget, philosophy of ministry, values, and long-range strategy. Then the staff makes the day-to-day decisions regarding how money is spent within the approved budget, what ministries to begin and stop, and whom to hire and fire within the staff.

Adjust Staff Organization

The senior pastor must decide either to continue a direct management connection with the larger church staff or to delegate staff management to an executive pastor. If a senior pastor desires to travel a great deal, speak at conferences, write for publication, or spend greater time in preparation for sermons, it is common for the church to call an executive pastor to take care of the on-campus ministry. However, if the pastor would rather stay connected to the pastoral staff, it is common for the church to form a smaller executive staff team. Whatever direction the pastor chooses to go, a change in staff organization normally takes place when the church is between about 1,200 and 1,500 in size.

Be Team Builders

The staff must transition from being "practitioners" to "team builders," from being on the team to *leading* a team. Moving beyond 1,500 requires a staff that is able to build ministry teams rather than simply being able to do ministry themselves. When a church is smaller, it will most often call staff members who are good at doing ministry—they are excellent practitioners. However, for a church to grow larger than 1,500, it usually takes a number of key staff members who are able to build ministry teams that will assist in the growth and expansion of the ministry program. For example, a small church may hire a worship pastor who will lead the worship services, but for a church to grow larger than 1,500, a worship pastor must be able to build several worship teams that will be available to lead numerous worship services. In fact a worship leader may not actually lead any worship services but he or she must be able to build a worship ministry using multiple worship teams.

> For a church to grow larger than 1,500, it usually takes a number of key staff members who are able to build ministry teams that will assist in the growth and expansion of the ministry program.

The difficulty comes in determining what to do with staff members who are incapable of building teams that will take the church to the next level of ministry. The church has just a few choices. It can provide training to help a pastor learn to build teams, it can assist staff members in moving to other churches, or it can realign the staff members in a different configuration so that those who are incapable of building teams are no longer expected to do so but are put on someone else's team.

Be a Church of Small Groups

The church must move from being a church *with* small groups to a church *of* small groups. Providing care for the growing number of church participants is perhaps the major challenge of taking it to the next level in a church larger than 1,500 people. The number of people being served in a centralized church is so large that it is commonplace for people to get somewhat lost in the crowd. If a church relies solely on the pastoral staff to provide care for all church members, it will fail. The only practical way to provide care is to give every person in the church this responsibility. If everyone is involved in caring for each other, there is high probability that the care provided will be good and consistent.

Think beyond the Local Church

A centralized church must recruit board members who think globally not just locally. This means they think beyond their local church, which is essential because a church of more than 1,500 will have a ministry impact that reaches beyond the local church's neighborhood. If the church's impact is to continue in this larger sphere of influence, it will take a board that is able to think beyond the local church's ministry.

What's Happening?

1. Is your church a centralized church? What insights make you say that it is or isn't?
2. What characteristics of the centralized church can you identify in your church ministry?
3. What key points of transition outlined in this chapter might you be able to make to take your church to the next level?

15

The Decentralized Church

1,500-Plus Worshipers

Try a little harder than you want to; aim a little higher than you think possible.

Art Linkletter

"I'll bet that growing larger than a couple of thousand people gets a lot more difficult," Phil said.

"I'm sure," Wes agreed. "I haven't served in a church that large but I've known several people who pastored churches with more than 2,000 worshipers and have an idea of some of the struggles they've faced."

"I didn't think there were really many churches with more than 2,000 people," Mike said. "Do you think there are?"

"From what I know, you're right, Mike," Wes agreed. "I've read that less than 2 percent of all churches have more than 2,000 in worship attendance."

"But they get all the press!" Phil laughed.

"That's for sure," Mike agreed. "You don't see many stories about smaller churches in the newspapers."

"No, you don't," Wes smiled. "While that may be a little discouraging, there is a lot we can learn from the mega-churches. They do an excellent job of evangelism, as well as connecting people to the church. From what I've been able to discover from my friends, larger churches do a much better job at placing members in ministry than smaller churches."

"Is that true?" Phil looked puzzled. "I always thought people attended megachurches just to hide out."

Wes chuckled. "That may be the perception but it's not fact. I've found that larger churches actually do a better job of getting people into ministry. For example, last year I attended a megachurch in my wife's hometown. While talking to the lady who directed the church's nursery, I found out she needed a minimum of 235 workers each week. The thing that still amazes me is that she is able to find that many nursery workers. I have trouble finding four or five nursery workers, but that church is able to recruit, train, and place more than 200 workers in the nursery each week. And, that's just one of their ministries!"

"Wow, I never thought of it that way," Phil said.

"Me either, but it's true that the megachurches are excellent in building systems to welcome and involve new people."

Churches that grow larger than 1,500 are called mega-churches. Technically, megachurches are defined as those with more than 2,000 in worship attendance, but once a church starts moving beyond 1,500 worshipers, it is certainly in megachurch territory.

Currently it is estimated that only about 1 or 2 percent of all churches in the United States fall into this category.[1] Such churches do, however, offer excellent examples of how to do ministry in effective ways. For the most part, mega-churches tend to be more creative than small churches, and they do a much better job of developing processes for reaching new people, winning them to Christ, and involving them in discipleship.

The fact that there are so few churches found at this size indicates the difficulty of taking a church to this level of ministry. The following are some of the characteristics of churches found at this largest size.

Characteristics

Churches tend to centralize ministry as they grow beyond 800 in size, but then as they grow beyond 1,500 in worship attendance, they begin to notice that the centralization of ministry becomes a straitjacket that keeps the ministry from growing larger. The divisional approach to organizational structure that worked to help the church grow from 800 to 1,500 in size actually becomes a barrier to further growth. Church leaders begin to refer to the divisional structure as silos. This term implies that the various divisions develop thick walls around them that effectively stop communication and cooperation from taking place. If a church is to go to the next level, it must break down walls between ministries and move toward a decentralized approach. In this structure anyone in ministry is given freedom to communicate and work across all ministry arenas to get the work done.

With the decentralizing of ministry, the management structure of the entire church becomes more matrixlike. The rigid silo approach to structure that provided clear lines of authority and ability to make decisions (see chart in previous chapter) must gradually give way to an interconnected approach, that looks much like a spider web (see figure 39 on page 171). Church leaders give permission for anyone in a ministry position to move across programs to communicate or partner with those in different areas of ministry to empower effective and fruitful ministry work.

FIGURE 39
Matrixlike Structure

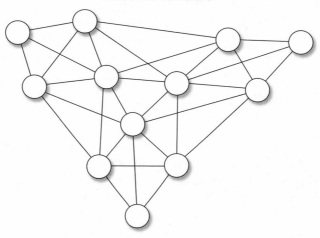

The matrixlike structure effectively pushes ministry decision making down to the lowest level, which allows for those actually doing the ministry to make the decisions that affect their area of service. By the time a church reaches 1,500 in size, it will normally employ either an executive pastor or a small executive team who oversee the entire church ministry. The complexity becomes so great in larger churches that it takes more than one or two people to oversee the ministry effectively. Thus the executive leadership develops a staff team made up of multiple staffs. To understand this dynamic, it will be helpful to consider how staff teams develop as a church grows larger in size. In the managerial church (200–400) there is often a small staff of three or four people (see figure 40 on page 172).

The matrixlike structure effectively pushes ministry decision making down to the lowest level, which allows for those actually doing the ministry to make the decisions that affect their area of service.

All of the staff members report to the single pastor, who is at the center of all ministry.

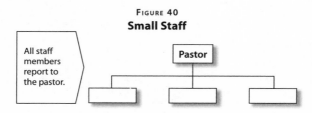

FIGURE 40
Small Staff

All staff members report to the pastor.

Pastor

As a church grows to the level of an organizational church (400–800), it further develops a multiple staff. There are two levels of staff and some staff members no longer report directly to the senior pastor but to other staff members

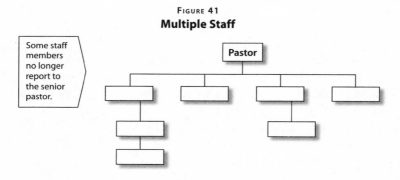

FIGURE 41
Multiple Staff

Some staff members no longer report to the senior pastor.

Pastor

Taking it to the level of 800–1,500 requires that a church develop a multiple-level staff, found at least at three different levels of the church organization. Two levels of staff report to other staff rather than to the senior pastor (see figure 42 on page 173).

By the time a church takes it over 1,500 in size, a team of multiple staffs develops. There is no longer just a single multiple staff; rather there are several multiple staffs found throughout the church structure (see figure 43 on page 173).

By the time a church has multiple staffs, it becomes clear that the senior pastor is a movement builder. Typically the

FIGURE 42

Multiple-Level Staff

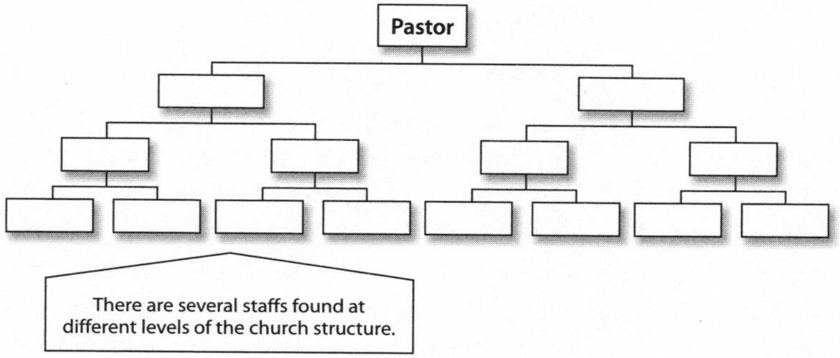
Pastor
There are several staffs found at different levels of the church structure.

FIGURE 43

Multi Staffs

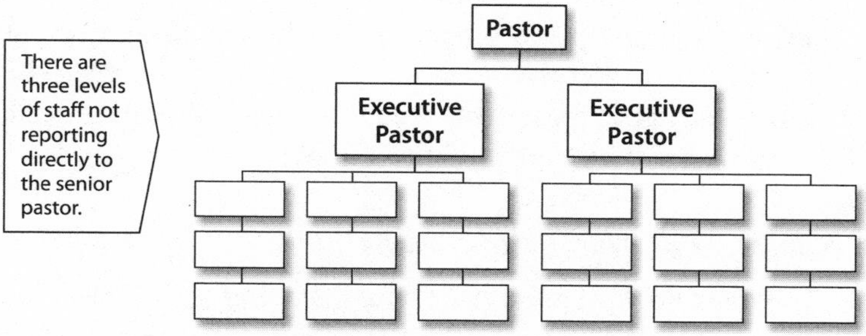
There are three levels of staff not reporting directly to the senior pastor.
Pastor
Executive Pastor
Executive Pastor

church ministry reaches a wide span of people and is often described as a congregation of congregations. Ministry impact is distributed regionally and perhaps is even felt across the nation or around the world. The pastor is in demand to speak, write, or counsel others and must make a decision on whether to concentrate his ministry in this one congregation or to expand ministry to those outside the local church.

Key Points of Transition

Taking a church beyond 1,500 requires a number of changes in the church's organizational structure. The following are some of the more crucial changes that must be made to reach the next plateau.

Add Executive Pastors

If a church reaches this level without an executive pastor, or perhaps with a single executive pastor, it is time to add additional executive-level pastors who are able to oversee the enlarging ministry. The most common arrangement is to place two executive pastors over the ministry, with one overseeing ministry staff and one overseeing administrative staff. This arrangement works well even for churches in the multiple thousands. However, whatever arrangement is employed, oversight of the complex ministry must be shared among executive staff members who are able to think, act, and plan for such a large ministry. It is crucial to separate program oversight and management oversight on the executive team. The executive team has to be more involved in coaching other staff leaders and doing strategic planning rather than being involved in day-to-day issues.

Select a Staff That Builds Teams

Ministry and staff personnel who have the capacity to take the various ministries to the next level must be selected. One of the most difficult aspects of leading a church beyond 1,500 worshipers is the realization that beloved staff members who got you to the current level will not be able to take you beyond it. This means some staff members will need to be replaced and/or redirected into other positions within the church structure. The key qualification in future staff members at the top staffing levels becomes an ability to build their own staff teams rather than simply working on or with the larger team.

Select Experienced Board Members

A similar challenge is faced in choosing board members. Some of the board members who helped the church reach its present level of ministry become road-blocks to an expanding ministry. While character qualifications continue to be of prime importance for board members, as well as staff members, it becomes increasingly important to select board members from among people who have led an organization or budget larger than that of the church. When the church board starts making decisions involving millions of dollars, members who cannot think in such large terms often become barriers to future growth.

> **When the church board starts making decisions involving millions of dollars, members who cannot think in such large terms often become barriers to future growth.**

Both the board and staff must become strategic about change. While smaller churches are able to change directions fairly fast, the larger church takes longer to initiate changes of direction. More time and global thinking are required to plan strategically for the church's future.

Add New Departments

New departments within the church must be established to enable the church to function well. For example, a tech department that establishes a computer network for communication becomes necessary as a church grows beyond 1,500 in size. With more staff comes the need to have a human resources department to handle benefits, hiring and firing, and a host of other staff-related issues.

Maintain the Church's Image

The church must become more intentional about managing the church "brand" by formalizing, communicating, and protecting the church's name and image in the community. Larger churches impact such a wide swath of people that their

175

name becomes extremely well-known. The leadership team must take great care in communicating what the church is and is not to the community and perhaps to the nation. Protecting the church's brand is a key task of the executive team.

A major aspect of brand management relates to the problem of maintaining authenticity. Some people automatically perceive of smaller churches as more authentic than larger ones. People just do not see how a large church that offers professional worship services, specialized ministry leaders, and expansive faculties can remain authentic. In the minds of some, the larger a church grows, the more watered down its brand.

Growth and authenticity are not incompatible. Authenticity is not a function of size but of a church's connection to four strands of meaning.

1. Authenticity comes from being connected to a place with a story. A church with a unique story becomes a place that people find authentic. All churches, but particularly larger ones, must be adept at telling their special story to help people connect to it as an authentic place.
2. Authenticity comes from being connected to people who are passionate. Churches that are able to motivate their people to be passionate about ministry are perceived as authentic.
3. Authenticity comes from being connected to a great purpose. This is where decentralized churches often shine, as they are able to envision and pursue captivating visions for the future.
4. Authenticity comes from being connected to values. The story that a church tells must align with its actions.

Thus an authentic church can be small, medium, or large. The issue is not its size but how well it connects to its story, passion, purpose, and values. With this definition of authenticity, a small church may actually be less authentic than a larger one. Yet as a church grows ever larger, the leaders must manage the brand to make certain it remains true to its history.

What's Happening?

1. Is your church a decentralized church? Why do you think you are at this level of ministry?
2. What characteristics of this size church do you see developing in your church?
3. Which of the five transition point challenges are you currently facing?

PART THREE

CHOICE
POINTS

16

Growth and Decline

Size Matters

It may be alright to be content with what you have, never with what you are.

B. C. Forbes

"Do you think it really matters how big a church is?" Phil loved to bring up this question from time to time in various conversations.

"Well, if you mean does God favor larger churches over smaller ones, I'd say no," Wes commented. "I like to adapt a comment once made by Abraham Lincoln that God must love smaller churches because he made so many of them."

"True, true," Mike concurred. "But the size of a church does matter. Each size has a different DNA."

"DNA?" Phil spoke up. "I'd never thought of it that way. We all have DNA that controls our development. Maybe churches have unique DNAs too. What do you think, Wes?"

"I don't know if I'd call it DNA, but my observations over the years point to each size of church being unique. As an example, when I pastored a small church, we often communicated to the entire congregation through the prayer chain. Every family or single person was connected to the prayer chain in some fashion, and we discovered that if we wanted to get a message to the entire congregation all we had to do was pass it along the prayer chain. A few years later, I tried to communicate through the prayer chain at a much larger church and found it didn't work. Too many people in my larger church were not connected to the prayer chain. Eventually we found it necessary to communicate through several different channels to get our message out to the entire church. So, if that's evidence of DNA, than the smaller church has a different one than a larger church."

"I've got another example," Mike broke in assuredly. "When my church was smaller we didn't have to plan very far in advance. Once we started a brand new ministry in about four weeks. A soccer mom suggested we offer a soccer clinic as a means to reach some of the families in our community. The idea caught fire, and we had it all planned and ready to go in slightly less than a month. That could never happen in my current church. We'd need to plan for at least a year in advance just to get it on the calendar. I often tell our people that when our church was smaller we were like a speedboat able to change direction quickly. Today we're more like an ocean liner, and we need much more lead time to change direction."

> **The smaller church is a network of inner-relationships; the larger church is a network of interrelationships.**

"So size does matter," Phil reluctantly noted.

"Yes, it does," Mike and Wes said in unison.

Leaders like to talk about a church's DNA and how it controls the growth and development of their church. In living organisms, DNA is the nucleic acid that contains the genetic instructions used in the design of all known life. Some compare DNA to a set of blueprints, a recipe, or a code, since it contains the directions to build an organism's cells. Thus a church's DNA carries the information that quietly guides the way a church is formed.

The Impact of Size

Part of understanding a church's DNA is recognizing the rules that appear to govern the growth, decline, and fruitfulness of social organizations. Although church growth is ultimately the work of God the Father (see 1 Corinthians 3), there are general relationships between a church's size, associations, and organization that have crucial implications for its growth. The following are a dozen essential facts that we have learned about the impact of a church's size on its DNA.

Numerous and Complex Relationships and Structure

The larger a church becomes, the more numerous and complex will be the relationships and organizational structure. For example, in a small group consisting of 10 people, there are 45 potential relationships. However, in a church of 100 people, there are 4,950 potential relationships. And in a church of 500, there are 124,750 potential relationships![1] This means that, as a church grows larger, the leaders sense the need to work harder at communication, long-range planning, and building unity.

> **The smaller the church, the more general its organization; the larger the church, the more specialized its organization.**

Reflecting on the needs of a growing church, Lyle Schaller explains: "It probably will need a more complex organizational structure."[2] He goes on to suggest that, as a church grows larger, it needs a longer time frame for planning, a heavier emphasis on outreach, and a greater reliance on large-group organizing principles.

The Importance of Smaller Units

The larger a church becomes, the more it must break down into midsized and smaller units to maintain care and communication. Carl George addressed this issue in his pace-setting book *Prepare Your Church for the Future*. George predicts: "All churches, no matter what their size, must deal with a certain organizational issue if they're to experience the ongoing, quality growth that stems from Christ's Great Commission to 'make disciples' (Matt. 28:18–20)."[3] Later George defines this certain organizational issue: "Churches find that each time they grow a little, their quality lessens, so they must scramble to implement a new organizational system geared to their current size."[4] As churches increase in size and in the number of relationships, it becomes increasingly difficult to provide care for all the people and to get them involved. George discovered that churches must become ever smaller as they grow ever larger. Thus the larger a church, or any organization, becomes, the more it must break down into smaller units to maintain an actable level of care for its members. When a church grows larger, an emphasis on small-group ministry is absolutely necessary if it hopes to maintain a positive flow of communication and pastoral care to all of its worshipers.

Specialized Roles and Functions

As a church becomes larger, it must develop specialized roles and functions and increase the total number of roles. Jethro's advice to Moses in Exodus 18 is the classic biblical illustration of this point. Observing the struggle of Moses to care for the concerns of the people of Israel, Jethro suggested that he break down the oversight into subdivisions of leaders. Jethro recommended that Moses select leaders of thousands, hundreds, fifties, and tens (see Exod. 18:21). Minor disputes among the people of Israel were handled at the lowest level, while major disputes were pushed farther up the path of leadership. Thus not only did Moses expand the number of leaders, but those at the different levels took on more specialized roles. Likewise as churches grow up and beyond each step or plateau, they must increasingly add additional leaders while expanding the types and functions of roles. In smaller churches, one person or group of people does all the evangelism, assimilation, and pastoral care. However, in larger churches these tasks become specialized, each performed by a trained leader, putting a premium on specialization, association, and cooperation.

> **The larger a church, or any organization, becomes, the more it must break down into smaller units to maintain an actable level of care for its members.**

Specialized Groups

When a church becomes large, its subgroups must become more specialized and diverse. When churches are small, they would normally offer a limited number and array of small-group studies. However, as churches grow larger, they begin offering an ever-growing number of specialized groups—12-step groups, support groups, task groups, and so on. As I've said before, this is tied to the issue of critical mass. For example, a smaller church may have only one or two families dealing with alcoholism. While the church leaders are no doubt concerned for the special needs of the two families, there is not sufficient critical mass to offer a small support group or specialized class for them. As a church grows larger, however, it will soon have a number of families dealing with alcoholism. With the increased critical mass, the church will be able to offer a support group and/or special needs class aimed directly at this particular concern.

Formalized Roles

The larger a church becomes, the more its roles are formalized, and the number of levels of lay and staff roles increases. When small churches begin adding staff members, it is quite common to use simple titles like associate pastor or assistant pastor or director of children's ministry. These are broad terms that help to identify the role and function of these staff members. However, as a church grows larger, the titling of each staff member becomes more specific and formal, such as associate pastor of assimilation, administrative pastor, or director of preschool. The formalization of the role and title narrows down the exact function that each person does in the performance of his or her role. The same occurs with lay roles and titles. Smaller churches may have elders and deacons, but larger churches have administrative elders, ruling elders, ministering elders, shepherding elders, and a host of other more specific titles and functions.

Methods of Communication

As a church grows, regular communication of its vision, values, mission, and philosophy of ministry is important so that everyone knows what the church is about. But maintaining unity of purpose and direction becomes difficult as a church grows larger. The increasing number of relationships means that the grapevine, which was used to communicate effectively when the church was smaller, no longer works. In addition, the natural process of communication means that some meaning is lost at every level on the communication chain.

At the top level of the communication chain, a message is shared with an expectation that the people will remem-

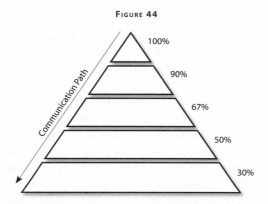

Figure 44

ber 100 percent of it. But as you can see, the second level of leadership actually catches only about 90 percent of the message. As the message is communicated farther down the various levels of church leadership, more and more of it is lost until fewer and fewer people understand it. At the third tier of leadership, only about 67 percent of the message is heard. By the fourth tier only 50 percent is received. When the communication reaches the congregation, only about 30 percent of the message is received.

In a relational church a message has to travel only one level to reach the entire congregation; this is the reason the grapevine works so well. Yet as can be seen in the illustration above, the decentralized church has numerous levels that a message must traverse before it reaches the entire congregation. Thus growing churches find that redundant systems must be put in place to ensure that all communication permeates throughout the entire church.

Key Influencers of Ministry Direction

In smaller relational churches, it is often the entire congregation that drives the decision-making process; the congregation desires a say in almost all decisions made on behalf of the church. Such an organizational approach to decisions can work very well because the church is small enough for its members to have a sufficient breadth of knowledge about the entire church ministry to make wise decisions.

The larger a church grows, the more the senior pastor and pastoral staff gain authority as the key influencers of ministry direction.

As a church grows, however, members of the congregation begin to realize they no longer have the breadth of understanding of the church program to make good discussions. When the church reaches the managerial size, many decisions are handed over to a board and various committees. And when a church moves through the organizational, centralized, and decentralized levels, the congregation and board gradually come to understand that only the senior pastor and members of the pastoral staff have enough knowledge of the total church ministry to make day-to-day functional decisions. The larger a church grows, the more the senior pastor and pastoral staff gain authority as the key influencers of ministry direction. The congregation of a large church expects and allows the senior pastor to have a vision for ministry and they adopt that vision.

Potential for Conflict

In a large church, there is more potential for conflict among various parts of the organizational system. The relational character of smaller churches allows for good communication and coordination of ministry functions. While smaller churches do experience conflict, there appears to be a greater opportunity for disharmony as the church grows, due to the increased difficulty in communicating with larger groups of people. Conflict arising from the use of facilities, distribution of finances, coordination of plans, and a host of other related issues becomes more probable as a church increases in size. Therefore the leadership of larger churches must focus on assisting subunits to relate well with each other and function with harmony.

The Need for Decentralized Ministry

When a church is small, it is possible for a single person to oversee, coordinate, and control its activities, but once a church moves from the relational church size to managerial size, it becomes increasingly impossible to do so. As leaders share ministry leadership with others, push caregiving and decision making down to the lowest levels of lay ministry—the church becomes increasingly decentralized in government and oversight.

Learning from Other Churches

The larger a church becomes, the more necessary it is that it learn from other churches of equal or greater size, even from churches of different theology, polity, or any number of identifiable aspects. The large size of a church is its primary definitive characteristic. Other than a church's cultural context, its size is the main determinant of its organization. Growing churches soon discover that fewer and fewer churches are available from which they can learn. Since most denominations and church associations are made up of smaller churches, a growing church may find very few churches in its own theological family with whom it will share common concerns and needs. Thus larger churches look to churches of their same size to learn how to take it to the next level.

The Need to Plan for the Future

A large church must look farther into the future and focus on issues and needs that are removed in time and space from its current situation. A small speedboat can be turned around in a very short space, but to turn an ocean liner around takes many miles and a longer time frame in which to do so. The same is true of churches. Smaller churches are like speedboats in that they can be turned very quickly if the pastor and people desire to do so. Larger churches, much like ocean liners, need much more time to communicate the necessity, the plan, and the procedure for turning in a new direction.

The same is true regarding a church's span of ministry impact. Generally, smaller churches focus on ministry needs close to home in their neighborhood, city, or state. Larger churches look to meet ministry needs in the nation and world due in part to greater resources and vision. To reach the next level, a church must solve problems in a smaller space before it can concern itself with issues in a larger space. This means that the larger the space (city, state, nation, world) and the longer the time (week, month, year, multiple years), the fewer churches that will be involved in solving problems at that level. Thus the leaders of larger churches must be increasingly more adept at strategic planning.

FIGURE 45

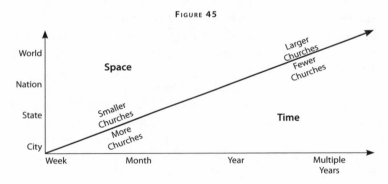

Innovation

As churches grow larger in size, they demonstrate economy-of-scale relationships; that is, a doubling of size requires less than a doubling of resources. For example, a small relational church can add a second worship service, and include more people, without needing to add a second worship leader. One worship leader can lead two or three different worship services, which allows the church to double or triple without increasing its cost for paying an additional worship pastor.

The opposite occurs with regard to creative output. The larger a church becomes, the more important it is that it continue to innovate. A phenomenon called super linear scaling[5] takes place regarding creativity—as a church increases in size, it expands its ability to innovate. Thus it is no surprise that most of the new ministry programs are designed, tested, and developed by larger churches rather than smaller ones. Not only are larger churches more innovative than smaller ones, it apparently is important that they continue to innovate. Geoffrey B. West, president of Santa Fe Institute in Santa Fe, New Mexico, declares, "In the absence of continual major innovations, organizations will stop growing and may even contract, leading to either stagnation or ultimate collapse. Furthermore, to prevent this, the time between innovations must decrease as the system grows."[6]

> **Understanding the dynamics of growth: interesting. Knowing where your church is going: priceless.**

Size Matters

The world has been in a race to build the tallest tower. For more than forty-one years the Empire State Building in New York City reigned as the tallest building in the world. Built in 1931 it stands 1,250 feet in height. In 2004 the Taipei 101 building was completed and is now one of the tallest in the world at 1,666 feet. Targeted for completion before 2010 are two new skyscrapers—the International Business Center in Seoul, Korea, is projected to top out at 1,902 feet, while the Burj Dubai in the United Arab Emirates will be 2,296 feet. Neither of these buildings will hold the record as the world's tallest building for long. The Burj Mubarak al-Kabir, a proposed skyscraper near Kuwait, would rise to 3,284 feet.

Unlike the race to build the tallest building, the purpose of *Taking Your Church to the Next Level* is not to help you build a church larger than the one down the street. It is, however, meant to assist you in understanding what is blocking the growth of your church and what you can do to see it reach a new level of impact.

Of course the congregational life cycle model and the congregational size model, both of which illustrate the growth of a congregation, have limitations. All churches are unique organisms and as such may not always fit the models as presented. A model is simply a way of looking at a complex system—in this case a local church. To some extent every model is imperfect, oversimplified, and unfinished. Even with their limitations, however, the life cycle and size models are helpful in providing snapshots of the threats and opportunities that are likely to fill a leader's viewfinder. Integrating the two models together provides a way to predict how soon a church will enter the danger zone. For example, a small church has the potential of falling into the dangerous red zone within two or three decades of existence (see chapter 9).

FIGURE 46
Smaller Church

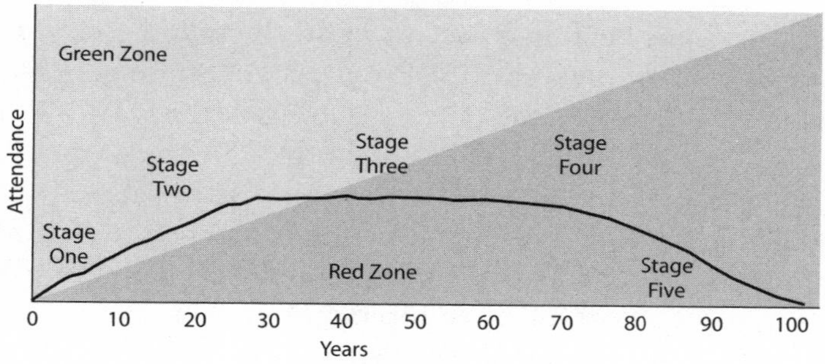

Depending on the strength of the early vision and other factors, a medium-sized church may remain in the green zone for four or five decades before reaching a point of decline.

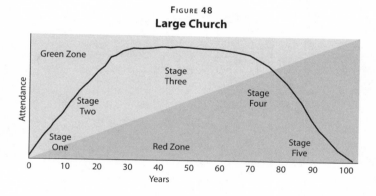

FIGURE 47
Medium-Sized Church

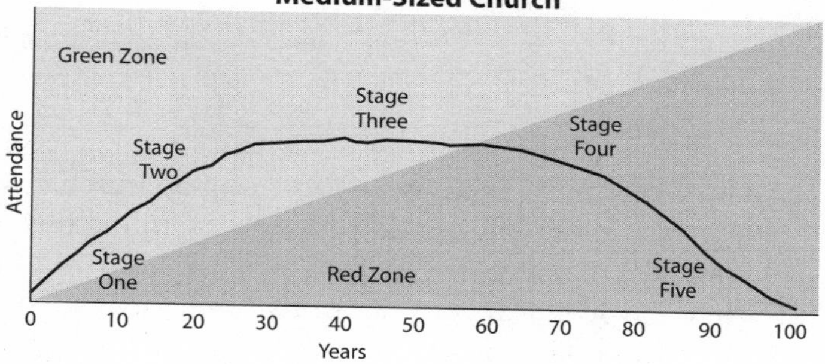

A larger church may see its strength last for six or seven decades before experiencing major stagnation and decline. The growth momentum, numerous resources, and high visibility may serve to keep the church in the positive green zone for much longer than smaller-sized churches.

FIGURE 48
Large Church

By looking at both the size model and life cycle model, it is easy to see that the larger a church becomes, the more likely it is to maintain a healthy ministry for a longer period of time.

Size does matter. It is clear that the nature of all organisms, including churches, is to change as they increase in size; this is true of the churches we love and serve. As we continue to grapple with the challenges of understanding and applying

193

church-size strategies to impact our churches, our efforts will have far-reaching effect.

What's Happening?

1. Which of the twelve facts concerning a church's size described in his chapter do you see developing in your church?
2. What do you feel are the two or three major challenges your church is facing as it seeks to grow to the next level?
3. In very practical words describe what you think must happen for your church to reach the next level of its ministry?

17

Reaching Your Growth Point

The point of greatest resistance is when we first begin to act on the truth. From that point on, resistance gradually diminishes.

Paul Evanson

"I can't tell you two how helpful this conversation has been," Mike said while glancing at Wes and Phil. "I came in here today a little discouraged, but just talking things over with you has helped me see things more clearly."

"Great!" Wes nearly shouted. "That's what friends are for, right?"

"I'm in total agreement," Phil added. "In my mind, this has been one of the best times of discussion we've ever had together. I know I've learned a lot today."

"So, what's our take-home value?" Wes inquired. "We all agree that there are predictable life cycle and size patterns that all churches face, but what is our role in all of this?"

"I'd say our job is to help a church just to be healthy," Phil offered.

"I'm not sure I'm totally in tune with you, Phil," Wes said. "I think it goes beyond just health to fitness."

"Okay, explain what you mean," Mike demanded in mock disgust.

"What I mean is, a church can be healthy but not fit. Let me use myself as an example. I'm healthy, but I'm surely not fit. No way could I run a mile without being very winded. In a similar way, I think there are a lot of churches that are healthy, by which I mean they have no major problems or illnesses, but they are not fit. They are not doing what a church should be doing."

"What should they be doing?" Phil questioned.

"They should be maximizing ministry both inside *and* outside the church," Wes said firmly. "I've found that when churches focus on being healthy they most often are talking about spiritual growth of their own people. But I think fitness relates to effectively reaching people who are outside of a church. A fit church is one that balances the spiritual growth of its own people while simultaneously reaching new people for Christ."

"Well, then, I want a fit church rather than a healthy church," Mike commented while looking at his watch. "But this will have to be a conversation for another day."

The growth point is that place in the life cycle of a congregation where maximum ministry occurs both inside (spiritual growth) and outside (spiritual birth).

Throughout this book I have suggested that there are predictable patterns and cycles that churches face as they seek to be everything that God intends them to be. There is a time or a point in the life cycle of every church when things seem to fit together so well that the ministry moves along with each and every aspect of the church's ministry working at its best. I call this point of time a church's *growth point*. Thus the growth point is that place in the life cycle of a congregation where maximum ministry occurs both inside (spiritual growth) and outside (spiritual birth). Whenever a church finds itself in the balanced position of seeing a significant number of new people coming to faith in Christ and believers already in the church growing in their spiritual lives, it is at its growth point.

A church's growth point is typically located at the transition point between the growth phase and the maturity phase of its life cycle.

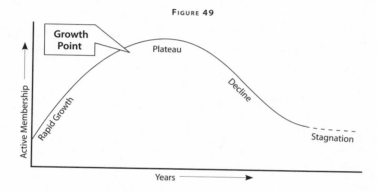

FIGURE 49

At this juncture of its life cycle, the church will experience the greatest excitement and energy level. This is when people are accepting Christ and believers are experiencing spiritual growth, and the power expanding from this growth point is so strong that it regularly propels the church forward for an additional twenty to forty years of effective ministry before decline eventually begins.

It is the job of church leaders to keep the church at its growth point for as long as possible, or to return the church to a growth point after it has been passed. When church leaders are able to return the church to its growth point, a new life cycle begins, which can last for another twenty-plus years. However, if a church never returns to its growth point, it will continue with much less vitality, eventually losing so much ministry vigor that it closes its doors or slides into a time of mere survival.

In considering how to guide a church to reach its growth point, I find good insight in the wisdom of Nehemiah. As you will recall, Nehemiah sought to rebuild the walls of Jerusalem during the time of King Artaxerxes. It was a daring venture, since the king had decreed that no work on the walls could be done (see Ezra 4:17–24). Adding to the challenge was the opposition Nehemiah faced from surrounding groups who did not want the walls rebuilt. What did Nehemiah do? He tells us: "We prayed to our God, and because of them set up a guard against them day and night" (Neh. 4:9). Nehemiah kept a spiritual focus ("we prayed to our God") while managing the process (we "set up a guard").

Keep a Spiritual Focus

Keeping a spiritual focus requires that we do at least three things.

Focus on Prayer

First, take time to pray. When the first century church faced the challenge of organizational change, they prayed. Luke tells us that a problem arose in the distribution of food to widows (Acts 6:1–6). This was an administrative problem that was created due to the growth of the church. The answer was to put a new level of leadership in place that could oversee the distribution of the food. The apostles and people prayed before, during, and following the appointment of the new leaders. Remember: we lose our vision if we stop praying.

Focus on the Big Picture

Keep the big picture in view. One of the classic stories from the Old Testament illustrates this concept well. When the

Arameans plotted to capture Elisha, as recorded in 2 Kings 6:8–17, his servant got up early in the morning and was shocked to see an army with horses and chariots surrounding the city. Frightened, the servant asked Elisha what to do. Elisha answered, "Do not fear, for those who are with us are more than those who are with them" (v. 16). While the servant focused narrowly on the visible army surrounding the city, Elisha had the big picture in view. He knew God had his own army of horses and chariots of fire protecting them (see v. 17). Remember: we lose our vision when we focus too narrowly.

Focus on God

Finally, we must focus on God. Ultimately it is God who causes a church to grow. Paul reminds us in 1 Corinthians 3:6 that God causes the growth. Christ promised in Matthew 16:18: "I will build My church." We do not build our church. It is God's job and he has promised to do it. Remember: we lose our vision when we focus on ourselves and our problems.

Manage the Process

While it is God who ultimately causes a church to grow, we should also remember that he normally acts only with our involvement. Paul makes it clear that we are God's fellow workers, planting and watering in preparation for God's work. The bottom line is God usually works as we work. He brings growth as we prepare the soil of our church for his creative power. Managing the process requires the following.

Keep the Vision Alive

First, keep the vision alive. It is important that we review the vision of our church daily. The problems, criticisms, and struggles we face may overpower our vision if we do not keep

199

it as our focus. Remember: vision is an inside job. It must live in us before it will be lived in our people.

Share the Vision

Share your vision with people every day. My advice is to talk about your vision with at least one person a day. Your conversation does not have to be extensive, but whenever you get a chance, bring up some aspect of the church's vision. Remember: people buy into your vision when they buy into you. As you talk with people, not only do they get to know your vision but also they get to know you. If your vision is thriving within you, it will spill out in conversation with others.

Win People to the Vision

If you are to realize the vision, you will need to recruit a support team. As you share your vision with people, be on the lookout for those who resonate with you. When you find someone who believes in you and your vision, invite him or her to begin spending time with you each week in prayer and thinking about how to accomplish the vision. Over the course of six to twelve months, you will likely put together a team of about fifteen people who are supportive of the vision. Remember: if someone wants to run, run with him or her. If someone wants to walk, walk with him or her. But, if someone wants to sit, find someone else!

Nurture the Vision

One way to nurture the vision is to host a quarterly vision meeting. Every three months pull your leaders together for a time of training and vision casting. Carl George suggests organizing around the concepts of vision, huddle, and skill. The meeting should be no longer than ninety minutes. Open with a short message of about twenty minutes, motivating leaders to remember the vision. Then divide the leaders into small huddle groups of three to five people. Ask each person to share what is working in his or her area of ministry and then what is not working. Encourage each huddle to work together, exhorting one another, sharing information, finding solutions, and praying. Huddle time should take about thirty minutes. Following the huddle time, bring the leaders back into the large group for training in particular skills or perhaps to hear stories of how people are being reached through specific ministries.

> **If someone wants to run, run with him or her. If someone wants to walk, walk with him or her. But, if someone wants to sit, find someone else!**

Help People Claim the Vision

Preach on the vision every other week. I do not mean a pastor should devote an entire sermon to the vision every other week but that some mention of the vision must be woven into the pastor's message. Since the average person forgets the vision within two weeks, it is critical to remind the congregation of it often. Simply preaching on the vision of the church once or twice a year will not infuse it in the congregation's memory.

Remember the Past

Unless your church is a brand-new church plant, you have a past. One of the unique challenges of taking a church to the next level is maintaining the old ministry while moving into the future. Whatever the ministry was like in the past, it worked well for many years and will be remembered fondly by those who experienced the height of its success. So the current leadership should be careful to praise the past while also leading the church to embrace a new way of doing ministry.

Improve the Present

While planning for the future, we must be improving the present. A leader cannot ignore the church's present ministry and focus only on the future. Most people are in the church because of the present ministry, which will of necessity be continued for a number of years. Obviously it is unwise to ignore what is already in place. Work must be done on two fronts—past and future—to insure the support of everyone concerned.

Work with Those Who Support the Vision

God never leaves himself without a faithful remnant. Thus, even in the most difficult situations, there are a few people whom God has prepared to assist in turning the church around. Find these people and work with them to help you take the church to the next level.

New people are often points of life because they bring fresh insights, knowledge of new models, and creative experiences to bear on your growth strategies. Adding new leaders at a rate of 10 percent each year goes a long way in keeping a church vibrant. If you want your church to remain the same, keep recycling leaders. If you want your church to change, find a way to involve new leaders.

Adjust to the Needs of the Congregation

To manage the process of growth, the leadership approach will need to be adjusted along the way. As we have seen, each stage of the congregational life cycle calls for a different approach to leadership, so growing from one plateau to another requires pastors and lay leaders to develop new leadership skills. For a church to make it to a new level of ministry, leaders must improve their knowledge and practice. Great leaders adjust their leadership style to the needs of their organization.

Make the Right Choices

Choices are important because they lead to results. For the most part, churches are small because they have made choices over the years to remain small. Medium-sized churches have decided to stay medium-sized, and larger churches have grown due to their decisions. Leith Anderson reminds us: "Everyone chooses. Some choose with the future in mind, and others choose with the present in the center of their focus. Even some choose with the past, or rather returning to the past, as the goal. Even those who do not choose with a specific goal in mind make choices and those choices determine their future!"[1]

When a church advances along its life cycle and moves up in size, it encounters numerous times when choices have to be made. These choice points are a time of transition. If wrong decisions are made, the church will likely plateau or decline. If correct decisions are made, the potential increases for the church to grow. Each chapter of this book has offered insights and ideas regarding the threats a church encounters, as well as the opportunities it has for growth and vitality. Each chapter recounts the choices that churches need to make to take it to the next level. These are the choices you must make.

Taking It to the Next Level

Using the Choice-Making Grid below, answer the following key questions:

1. Where is your church on the life cycle? Mark with an X the spot where your church is today based on its current worship attendance and age.
2. In what zone would you place your church today? Red or Green?
3. Based on what you've discovered about your church today, what do you need to do to take your church to another level?

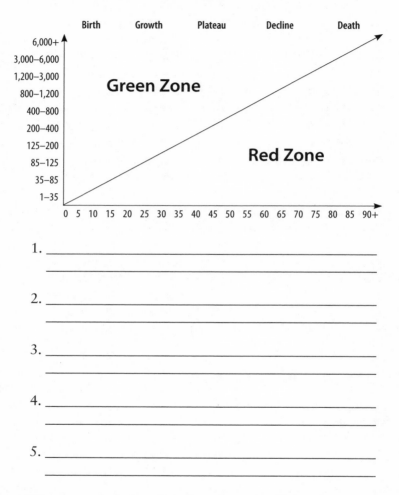

FIGURE 50
Plan Ahead

1. _____

_____

2. _____

_____

3. _____

_____

4. _____

_____

5. _____

_____

Wherever your church is found on the chart above, you have choices to make. There is no guarantee of success, but choosing well will position your church to take it to the next level of fruitful ministry. Making unwise choices will normally result in your church either remaining where it is or suffering decline in the years ahead. The choices are yours to make. Your church is at a choice point today, and your choices will determine its future. What choices will you make? Will you choose for growth or plateau or decline?

Appropriate Learning

Since you have read this far, you are one of those rare individuals who realize the importance of learning. To survive, no, to prosper in today's complex and complicated world of ministry, an individual, an organization, and even a church must focus on learning.

Traditionally church leaders practice a pattern of *maintenance learning*, which is the acquisition of fixed methods, rules, and processes for dealing with known and recurring situations. This type of learning is valuable since many of the challenges church leaders encounter on a day-to-day basis are not new, but issues all church leaders have faced in the past. For example, leaders have always struggled to welcome and connect newcomers to church. This issue is not a new one, and there are numerous fixed methods, rules, and processes that have been developed to deal with this recurring situation. Learning better ways for connecting guests to a church is maintenance learning. It enhances our ability to solve problems that appear repeatedly.

It is imperative, however, that we use a different type of learning in times of turbulence and change, such as we are now going through. The type of learning that can bring change, renewal, and problem solving is called *innovative learning*. Innovative learning is the preparation of individuals and organizations to anticipate, participate, and creatively solve the problems of both the present and the future. There are three primary features of innovative learning. First, we must *anticipate* problems, which means preparing people for possible contingencies and "what if" scenarios before they actually occur. Innovative learning requires leaders to use forecasting, simulations, models, and various scenarios to prepare their followers for the future. Second, we must encourage others to *participate* in finding solutions. This means adopting an attitude of cooperation, dialogue, and empathy. It involves keeping communication open while testing operating processes, values, and practices. Third, we must *creatively solve* the problems we anticipate, which requires problem detecting, problem understanding, and problem solving. Reliance on old methods, rules, and processes (maintenance learning) is not sufficient to answer many of today's challenges.[2]

In *Taking Your Church to the Next Level* I have incorporated both maintenance and innovative learning. Some of the insights and ideas found herein are based on fixed principles and processes, while others are innovative in nature. The tension created by the pressure to lead a church through the stages of its life cycle and plateaus of growth stimulates innovative learning. Such learning is a lifelong process.

Now get started applying the valuable lessons, ideas, and concepts you've discovered in this book, and you will be well on the way to taking your church to the next level.

Notes

Chapter 1 What Got You Here Won't Get You There

1. David O. Moberg, *The Church as a Social Institution: The Sociology American Religion* (Englewood Cliffs, NJ: Prentice-Hall, 1962).

2. Ibid., 119.

3. Robert D. Dale, *To Dream Again* (Nashville: Broadman Press, 1981)

4. Geoffrey B. West, "Innovation and Growth: Size Matters," *Harvard B Review* 85 no. 2 (February 2007): 34–35.

5. Larry E. Greiner, "Evolution and Revolution as Organizations Gro *vard Business Review* (May–June 1998), 55–67.

6. Lyle E. Schaller, *The Very Large Church: New Rules for Leaders (* Abingdon, 2000), 27.

Chapter 2 St. John's Syndrome

1. Ichak Adizes, "Organizational Passages: Diagnosing and Trea' Problems of Organization," *Organizational Dynamics* (Summer 1

2. Ichak Adizes, *Corporate Lifecycles: How and Why Corpora' Die and What to Do about It* (Paramus, NJ: Prentice Hall, 1988)

3. Ibid., 2.

4. Ibid., 202.

5. It is not the purpose of this book to analyze the corporate of Adizes. However, for the reader who is seriously interested in reading about organizational life cycles, it is highly recommende read Adizes's book mentioned above, as well as *Managing Cor* (Paramus, NJ: Prentice Hall, 1999).

207

6. Moberg was not the first to observe the presence of a church life cycle. He adapted his own perspectives from four other sociologists who published similar ideas between 1946 and 1948. See Moberg's *The Church as a Social Institution*, 118 (note 64).

7. Moberg, *The Church as a Social Institution*, 118.

8. Ibid., 119.

9. H. Richard Niebuhr first addressed this topic of how denominations develop. See H. Richard Niebuhr, *The Social Sources of Denominationalism* (Hamden, CT: Shoe String Press, 1954).

10. Elmer Towns used Moberg's sociological cycle of church growth while studying rapidly growing churches in the early 1970s. See Elmer Towns, *America's Fastest Growing Churches* (Nashville: Impact Books, 1972), 156.

11. Win Arn, "Is Your Church in a Mid-life Crisis?" *The Win Arn Growth Report* 7 (Pasadena, CA: Institute for American Church Growth, 1985), 1–2.

12. Robert D. Dale, *To Dream Again* (Nashville: Broadman, 1981).

13. Martin F. Saarinen, *The Life Cycle of a Congregation* (Bethesda, MD: The Alban Institute, 1986).

Chapter 3 The Emerging Church

1. I use the term *emerging church* for a new church plant. It should not be confused with the terms *emerging* or *emergent*, often used today to signal postmodern forms of the church.

Chapter 4 The Growing Church

1. Twenty to twenty-five years is a general time span for churches to reach their maximum size, based on observations of churches in the United States. As might be expected, some churches reach their largest size faster, and others take longer than this norm. A study by Kenneth E. Crow on the Church of the Nazarene conducted in 1986 discovered that the average Nazarene church took forty-five years to reach the denominational average size. See Kenneth E. Crow, "The Life Cycle of Nazarene Churches," www.nazarene.org/ministries/administration/ansr/author/display.aspx (accessed August 31, 2008).

Chapter 7 The Dying Church

1. For an excellent resource describing when and how to close a church, see ‍tephen Gray and Franklin Dumond, *Legacy Churches* (St. Charles, IL: Church-‍mart Resources, 2009).

‍hapter 8 Leading through the Stages

1. Crow, "The Life Cycle of Nazarene Churches," 2.

2. Carl F. George was the first to use this model in 1983 when he was director ‍he Fuller Evangelistic Association. For further research, see Floyd Tidsworth *Life Cycle of a New Congregation* (Nashville: Broadman, 1992), 140.

Chapter 9 Growing through the Stages

1. The feedback loop concept is adapted from Dennis L. Meadows, Donella Meadows, and Jorgen Randers, *The Limits to Growth* (New York: Signet, 1972).

Chapter 10 Step Up to the Next Level

1. Greiner, "Evolution and Revolution as Organizations Grow," 56.

2. Henry Mintzberg, *The Nature of Managerial Work* (New York: Harper and Row, 1973), 104.

3. Henry Mintzberg, *Structure in Fives: Designing Effective Organizations* (Englewood Cliffs, NJ: Prentice-Hall, 1983), 124–26.

4. Theodore Caplow, *How to Run Any Organization* (New York: Holt, Rinehart and Winston, 1976), 178.

5. Ibid., 179.

6. Kurt H. Wolff, *The Sociology of Georg Simmel* (New York: The Free Press, 1950), 87–177.

7. Ibid., 87.

8. Ibid., 89–90.

9. Ibid., 93–95.

10. Ibid., 97–98.

11. Ibid., 116.

12. Moberg, *The Church as a Social Institution*, 270.

13. Ibid., 41.

14. Ibid., 219–20.

15. Paul E. Mott, *The Organization of Society* (Englewood Cliffs, NJ: Prentice-Hall, 1965), 49.

16. Ibid., 38–70.

17. Ronald L. Johnstone, *Religion and Society in Interaction: The Sociology of Religion* (Englewood Cliffs, NJ: Prentice-Hall, 1975), 106–7.

18. Ibid., 107–8.

19. Lyle E. Schaller, *The Pastor and the People*, rev. ed. (Nashville: Abingdon, 1986), 145–47.

20. Lyle E. Schaller, *Hey, That's Our Church!* (Nashville: Abingdon, 1975), 39–50.

21. Lyle E. Schaller, *Effective Church Planning* (Nashville: Abingdon, 1979), 29.

22. Lyle E. Schaller, *The Multiple Staff and the Larger Church* (Nashville: Abingdon, 1980), 27–35.

23. Lyle E. Schaller, *The Very Large Church: New Rules for Leaders* (Nashville: Abingdon, 2000), 27.

24. David A. Womack, *The Pyramid Principle of Church Growth* (Minneapolis: Bethany Fellowship, 1977), 15–17.

25. Bill M. Sullivan, *New Perspectives on Breaking the 200 Barrier* (Kansas City: New Start, 2005), 15.

26. Carl F. George, *Prepare Your Church for the Future* (Tarrytown, NY: Revell, 1991), 42–43.

27. Ibid., 51–52.

28. Ibid., 177.

29. Ibid., 54.

30. Ibid., 10.

31. Leadership Network, *Innovation 2007: Connecting Innovators to Multiply* (Dallas: Leadership Network, 2007), 35.

32. Carl F. George, *How to Break Growth Barriers* (Grand Rapids: Baker, 1993), 129.

33. Ibid., 129–64.

34. Elmer Towns, C. Peter Wagner, and Thom S. Rainer, *The Everychurch Guide to Growth: How Any Plateaued Church Can Grow* (Nashville: Broadman and Holman, 1998)

35. Gary L. McIntosh, *One Size Doesn't Fit All: Bringing Out the Best in Any Size Church* (Grand Rapids: Baker, 1999).

36. Michael Fletcher, *Overcoming Barriers to Growth* (2003; reprint, Minneapolis: Bethany House, 2005), 20.

37. Kevin E. Martin, *The Myth of the 200 Barrier* (Nashville: Abingdon, 2005), 11.

38. Mark Driscoll, *Confessions of a Reformission Rev* (Grand Rapids: Zondervan, 2006), 28.

39. David B. Vasquez, "Staffing the Growing Megachurch" (DMin diss., Bethel University, 2006), 122–24.

40. My understanding is that the primary purpose of the church is to make disciples based on the Great Commission as found in Matthew 28:18–20. A faithful church, therefore, will be one that is growing numerically by making countable disciples, i.e., it will have more disciples this year than last. I am not implying that every church needs to be a large church; in fact, history demonstrates that very few churches will reach the size of a megachurch. However, I believe most churches can be more fruitful at making disciples than they are, and my desire is to help those who desire to grow.

41. Schaller, *Hey, That's Our Church!*, 42–43.

42. Ibid., 42–43.

43. For an excellent analysis of church size barriers see Vasquez, "Staffing the Growing Megachurch."

44. Some have suggested that the concept of growth barriers is a myth. Martin's statement that the 200 barrier is a myth, based on his reading of *The Tipping Point* (2002) by Malcolm Gladwell, is moot. While there clearly is no research data that supports a hard numerical barrier at 200, there is research data that supports numerical ranges, which can be spoken of as barriers. The same holds true for 400, 800, 1,200, or any other point on the chart in this chapter. See Martin, *The Myth of the 200 Barrier*.

45. Womack, *The Pyramid Principle of Church Growth*, 79.

Chapter 11 The Relational Church

1. See the author's earlier book *One Size Doesn't Fit All* for a breakdown of churches by size in the United States.

2. There are numerous variables, of course, including the giving level of worshipers, the location of the church, the financial support of a denomination, and the income needs of the pastor, just to name a few.

3. For specific information, see the author's book *Staff Your Church for Growth* (Grand Rapids: Baker, 2000), and David Vasquez's 2006 dissertation, "Staffing the Growing Megachurch."

4. For information on how to add a second worship service, see Charles Arn, *How to Start a New Service* (Grand Rapids: Baker, 1997).

Chapter 15 The Decentralized Church

1. See the author's book *One Size Doesn't Fit All* for a breakdown of churches by size.

Chapter 16 Growth and Decline

1. There is a mathematical formula that can be used to calculate how many potential relationships are possible given a certain number of people in a church. If n is the number of people, then $\frac{n(n-1)}{2}$ equals the total number of possible relationships.

2. Lyle E. Schaller, *The Middle-Sized Church* (Nashville: Abingdon, 1985), 129.

3. George, *Prepare Your Church for the Future*, 42.

4. Ibid., 43.

5. West, "Innovation and Growth," 35.

6. Ibid.

Chapter 17 Reaching Your Growth Point

1. Leith Anderson, *Dying for Change* (Minneapolis: Bethany House, 1990), 13.

2. I am indebted to and have adapted ideas on learning from A. G. "Buzz" Bainbridge, former vice president of Carlson Learning Company.

Further Reading

Worth a Look

Adizes, Ichak. *Corporate Lifecycles*. Paramus, NJ: Prentice Hall, 1988.

———. *Managing Corporate Lifecycles*. Paramus, NJ: Prentice Hall, 1999.

———. "Organizational Passages: Diagnosing and Treating Life Cycle Problems of Organizations." *Organizational Dynamics*, Summer 1979, 3–24.

Arn, Charles. *How to Start a New Service*. Grand Rapids: Baker, 1997.

Blau, Peter M. *The Structure of Organizations*. New York: Basic Books, 1970.

Blau, Peter M., and Richard Schoenheer. "Decentralization in Bureaucracies." In Mayer N. Zald, ed., *Power in Organizations*. Nashville: Vanderbilt University Press, 1971.

Caplow, Theodore. *How to Run Any Organization*. New York: Holt, Rinehart and Winston, 1976.

Driscoll, Mark. *Confessions of a Reformission Rev*. Grand Rapids: Zondervan, 2006.

Fletcher, Michael. *Overcoming Barriers to Growth*. Minneapolis: Bethany House, 2005.

Gaede, Beth Ann, ed. *Size Transitions in Congregations*. Bethesda, MD: Alban Institute, 2001.

George, Carl F. *How to Break Growth Barriers*. Grand Rapids: Baker Books, 1993.

————. *Prepare Your Church for the Future*. Tarrytown, NY: Revell, 1991.

Gladwell, Malcolm. *The Tipping Point: How Little Things Can Make a Big Difference*. Boston: Little, Brown, 2002.

Gray, Stephen and Franklin Dumond. *Legacy Churches*. St. Charles, IL: Churchsmart Resources, 2009.

Greiner, Larry E. "Evolution and Revolution as Organizations Grow." *Harvard Business Review*, May-June, 1998: 55–67.

Hammond, Phillip E., et al. *The Structure of Human Society*. Lexington, MA: D.C. Heath, 1975.

Johnstone, Ronald L. *Religion and Society in Interaction: The Sociology of Religion*. Englewood Cliffs, NJ: Prentice-Hall, 1975.

Martin, Kevin E. *The Myth of the 200 Barrier*. Nashville: Abingdon, 2005.

Martindale, Don. *Institutions, Organizations, and Mass Society*. New York: Houghton Mifflin, 1966.

McIntosh, Gary L. *One Size Doesn't Fit All*. Grand Rapids: Revell, 1999.

Miller, Lawrence M. *Barbarians to Bureaucrats: Corporate Life Cycle Strategies*. New York: Fawcett Columbine, 1989.

Mintzberg, Henry. *The Nature of Managerial Work*. New York: Harper and Row, 1973.

————. *Structure in Fives: Designing Effective Organizations*. Englewood Cliffs, NJ: Prentice-Hall, 1983.

Moberg, David O. *The Church as a Social Institution: The Sociology of American Religion*. Englewood Cliffs, NJ: Prentice-Hall, 1962.

Mott, Paul E. *The Organization of Society*. Englewood Ciffs, NJ: Prentice-Hall, 1965.

Nanus, B., and S. M. Dobbs. *Leaders Who Make a Difference: Essential Strategies for Meeting the Nonprofit Challenge*. San Francisco: Jossey-Bass, 1999.

Saarinen, Martin F. *The Life Cycle of a Congregation*. Bethesda, MD: The Alban Institute, 1986.

Schaller, Lyle E. *Effective Church Planning*. Nashville: Abingdon, 1979.

———. *Growing Plans: Strategies to Increase Your Church's Membership*. Nashville: Abingdon, 1983.

———. *Hey, That's Our Church*. Nashville: Abingdon, 1975.

———. *The Middle-Sized Church*. Nashville: Abingdon, 1985.

———. *The Multiple Staff and the Larger Church*. Nashville: Abingdon, 1980.

———. *The Pastor and the People*. 1973. Reprint, Nashville: Abingdon, 1986.

———. *The Small Church IS Different!* Nashville: Abingdon, 1982.

———. *The Very Large Church: New Rules for Leaders*. Nashville: Abingdon, 2000.

Sullivan, Bill M. *New Perspectives on Breaking the 200 Barrier*. Kansas City: New Start, 2005.

Towns, Elmer, C. Peter Wagner, and Thom S. Rainer. *The Everychurch Guide to Growth: How Any Plateaued Church Can Grow*. Nashville: Broadman and Holman, 1998.

Vasquez, David B. "Staffing the Growing Megachurch." DMin dissertation. Bethel University, 2006.

West, Geoffrey B. "Innovations and Growth: Size Matters." *Harvard Business Review* 85, no. 2 (February 2007): 34–35.

Wolf, Kurt H. *The Sociology of Georg Simmel*. New York: The Free Press, 1950.

Womack, David A. *The Pyramid Principle of Church Growth*. Minneapolis: Bethany Fellowship, 1977.

Gary L. McIntosh is an internationally known author, speaker, consultant, and professor of Christian Ministry and Leadership at Talbot School of Theology, Biola University, in La Mirada, California. He has written extensively in the field of pastoral ministry, leadership, generational studies, and church growth.

Dr. McIntosh received his BA from Colorado Christian University in Biblical Studies, an MDiv from Western Conservative Baptist Seminary in Pastoral Studies, a DMin from Fuller Theological Seminary in Church Growth Studies, and a PhD from Fuller Theological Seminary in Intercultural Studies.

As president of the Church Growth Network, a church consulting firm he founded in 1989, Dr. McIntosh has served more than five thousand churches in eighty-eight denominations throughout the United States and Canada. In 1995 and 1996 he served as president of the American Society for Church Growth. He edits the *Growth Points* newsletter (formerly *Church Growth Network*) and served as editor of the *Journal of the American Society for Church Growth* for fourteen years.

Services Available

Gary L. McIntosh speaks to numerous churches, nonprofit organizations, schools, and conventions each year. Services available include keynote presentations at major meetings, seminars and workshops, training courses, and ongoing consultation.

For a live presentation of the material found in *Taking Your Church to the Next Level* or to request a catalog of materials or other information on Dr. McIntosh's availability and ministry, contact:

Church Growth Network
PO Box 892589
Temecula, CA 92589-2589
951-506-3086
Email: cgnet@earthlink.net
On the World Wide Web at:
www.churchgrowthnetwork.com

ALSO BY GARY L. MCINTOSH

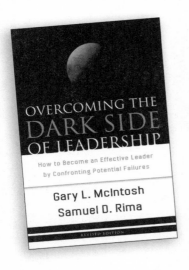

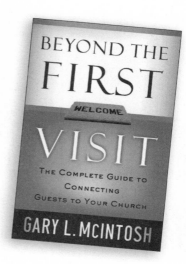

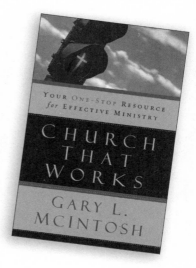

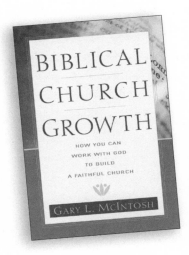

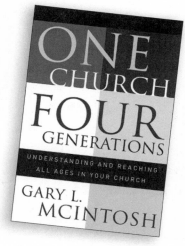

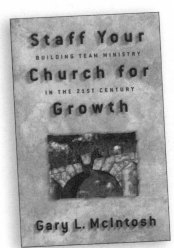

BakerBooks
a division of Baker Publishing Group
www.BakerBooks.com